Harriett Warner Ellis

Our Eastern Sisters and Their Missionary Helpers

Harriett Warner Ellis

Our Eastern Sisters and Their Missionary Helpers

ISBN/EAN: 9783743386907

Manufactured in Europe, USA, Canada, Australia, Japa

Cover: Foto ©Lupo / pixelio.de

Manufactured and distributed by brebook publishing software (www.brebook.com)

Harriett Warner Ellis

Our Eastern Sisters and Their Missionary Helpers

OUR EASTERN SISTERS

AND

THEIR MISSIONARY HELPERS.

BY

HARRIETT WARNER ELLIS,

AUTHOR OF "DENMARK AND HER MISSIONS;" "TOILS AND TRIUMPHS; OR,
MISSIONARY WORK," ETC.

LONDON:
THE RELIGIOUS TRACT SOCIETY;
56 Paternoster Row, 65 St. Paul's Churchyard,
And 164 Piccadilly.

TO THE

Right Honourable the Countess-Dowager of Gainsborough,

THE LONG-TRIED FRIEND OF FEMALE MISSIONS,

This Little Work

IS, BY HER KIND PERMISSION,

DEDICATED

BY

THE AUTHOR.

INTRODUCTION.

HE object of this book is to trace the beginning of women's work in the Christian education of their neglected, ignorant sisters in the East.

It describes their past condition, and the strong prejudices which existed against any efforts to ameliorate that condition. It traces the means used for overcoming difficulties, and the remarkable way in which God put it into the hearts of those whom He had qualified, to enter into the doors which He Himself had opened. It gives a short history of the lives and deaths of some of these heroines.

In addition to ladies who are devoting their lives and fortunes to missionary work, there are now more than twelve societies in Great Britain, and about twenty in America, engaged in it. Besides the Female Education Society, the pioneer in the British field, there are now the Church of England Zenana Society, the Indian Female Normal School Society, the Established and Free Church of Scotland Societies, and the London, Wesleyan, and Baptist Ladies' Societies.

The latest, and perhaps most popular effort, is the Medical Mission in Zenanas, which, having been commenced by our American sisters, is now taken up by the ladies of the various missionary societies. An hospital and training school for ladies has been opened by Dr. G. De Gorrequer Griffith in Westminster. In a touching paper he has published on the subject he says: "Having personally become acquainted with the sad state of women in Mussulman and Oriental countries, I long to hasten to their relief by the *only* means left in our power, through the prejudices of caste and religion, the ministration of the lady medical missionary, for no medical man is allowed to approach the Zenana. Their cries ring in my ears. Asleep and awake I hear them say, 'Send over and help us.' The lady missionary is now not only acceptable in the Zenana, but eagerly yearned for."

The press now gives prominence to this work, as is proved by the following extract from a daily paper: "The Queen has expressed her interest in the efforts now being made to provide fully qualified medical women for India. Miss Manning, Hon. Secretary of the National Indian Association, has received a letter from General Ponsonby, stating that Her Majesty gladly countenances a proposal suggested by Mr. Keltridge, of Bombay, to raise, with the co-operation of natives of India, a guarantee fund for the benefit of women doctors willing to go out from this country to settle in India." The fact that our beloved Queen has shown her royal sympathy will doubtless draw the attention of many of our countrywomen to a subject on which thousands of them are in utter ignorance.

So far back as July, 1876, Mr. Cowper Temple, now Lord Mount-Temple, urged the claims of Her Majesty's Indian female subjects upon the House of Commons. In a remarkable speech he said: "It will be a moral as well as a medical advantage to these women; for it will assist the Government in civilising, enlightening, and Christianising the native women, to have a large body of medical women trained in England, to go forth to India to undertake this great work."

Madras has led the way, and degrees are now given to ladies from her medical college.

Whilst thankful for what has already been accomplished, the work is as yet only begun. Our field of influence is overpowering. To borrow the language of a native gentleman, as just reported in an Indian paper: "The light has begun to shine in our Zenanas, and everything is changed. Only get the *hearts* of our women, and you will get the *heads* of the men."

It is in the hope of leading many to aid in this

great work that this little volume has been compiled. Help is urgently needed from those who cannot personally enter upon it to aid in sending out more labourers. The poor weary inmates of these Eastern homes—estimated in number at forty millions—are, writes one, "immured like caged birds, beating their tired wings against the prison walls vainly, yet eagerly longing to know something of what is beyond, and to hear further of the faint whisper which has been borne in to them of a brighter life somewhere, they know not where." The Zenana, notwithstanding its attractive name, is often the most dingy, dirty part of the whole establishment.*

In addition to periodicals, reports, and Lives and Histories from all the missionary societies, of which the writer has availed herself largely, she is mainly indebted for facts as to the general condition of women, and especially widows, in India, to the valuable work of the well known Bengali author, "The Hindoos as they Are," by Shib Chunder Bose, who writes not as a Christian, but as an educated Hindu. As such, he would not be likely to disparage his people and their institutions.

* A striking confirmation of this fact is found in the recent "Life of Lord Lawrence," published while this was in the press. He says: "Sometimes a pair of half-naked slave-girls, with the marks of stripes upon their backs, would escape from the window of their gilded prison-house. . . . At the best they are ill-treated, and suicide was very common among them."

The caution cannot too often be repeated that statements concerning one part of the vast country of India, which are strictly true, are quite inapplicable to other parts.

As an instance, in some parts of South India women are allowed much freedom, and in one small State are treated with respect and deference, and even permitted to hold land.

The same remark applies to results; while the Miss Brandons, devoted workers of the Church of England Zenana Society, tell of "a splendid school of 40 Hindus and 30 Mohammedan girls, and more than 100 names down for Zenana visitation" at or near Masulipatam; Miss Schwartz, an equally earnest labourer of the Indian Female Normal School Society at Nasik, tells of some of the difficulties. While one poor Hindu widow exclaims, "Oh, how kind of you to come and see me, a poor despised woman, when everyone is unkind;" two of her pupils told of the beating in store for them, should their husbands find out what they had been hearing; while another, more resolved to hear the Bible lesson, added, "I know what to expect; one beating more or less will make no difference to me." The testimony of another energetic worker, Miss Sargent, of the Wesleyan Missionary Ladies' Society in Ceylon, is most cheering. They have so many really Christian girls in their schools, that a place has been set apart where the girls may retire for private prayer, and she adds : " They show their belief by their lives; I never now hear bad language, and we very seldom have quarrels. Before the holidays they begged for portions of Scripture to take home, ' that their parents and friends might learn to know about Jesus and love Him as they did.' We have the testimony also of happy deaths."

The prominence given to the workers connected with the Female Education Society arises from the fact that the writer has been associated with it almost from the beginning.

An account of the first twelve years' work was published by the late Mrs. Trumper, who, with Miss Hope of Carriden, acted as Hon. Secretaries to the newly-formed society. By the courtesy of Miss Adam, Mrs. Trumper's sister, permission has been given to draw from its pages much valuable information.

Unlike other kindred societies, it comprises within the sphere of its operations, not only India, but China, Japan, the Straits, Persia, Mauritius, the Levant, and South and West Africa.

Its work in Nazareth and Bethlehem alone should create interest in the heart of every Christian woman in the United Kingdom.

It includes the women of these countries, of all ages and ranks, from the high-born ladies, secluded in

Zenanas and harems, to the half-savage Kaffir and Negro. The aim of these lady workers is to impress on all the truths of the Gospel and knowledge of the Scriptures, and at the same time to educate and civilise. The means employed are the sending out, after careful training, well-qualified ladies as Zenana missionaries and school teachers, who in their turn train native women for the same work.

The following statistics, gleaned from the latest reports of the various societies, will give some idea of the scale on which the work is now being carried on, as far as this can be done by figures :—

Income for 1882.

Church of England Zenana Missionary Society,	£23,008
Normal School Society,	7,595
Church of Scotland,	4,464
Free Church of Scotland,	5,291
Society for Promoting Female Education in the East,	7,652
Wesleyan Ladies' Missionary Society,	3,600
London Mission Ladies' Society,	2,300
	£53,900

The total raised by the Female Education Society since its commencement amounts to £133,663. In addition to this, work to the amount of £4000 or £5000 yearly has been sent abroad for sale.

Before concluding this short introduction, the

writer would note two special points in the work to be recorded; they are its catholicity, and its supplementary character. It is as Christ's work, and not that of any section or party in His Church, that these records are given; and it is as woman's work for Him.

May He who condescended to say to a woman, "She hath done what she could," deign to accept this humble effort to extend the knowledge of His name among women!

CONTENTS.

	PAGE
INTRODUCTION,	vii

CHAPTER I.
INDIA—BENGAL PRESIDENCY.

Condition of Women in the East—Early Efforts to help them—Labours of Mrs. Marshman, Mrs. Pearce, and Mrs. Gogerly—Death of Mrs. Gogerly—Miss Cooke's Work in Calcutta—Miss Bird—American Female Missionary Societies—Founding of the Society for Promoting Female Education in the East—Recent Statistics of the Work in Calcutta, ... 1

CHAPTER II.
INDIA—ORISSA.

Ignorance about Orissa—Mrs. Buckley's Description—The Meriah Sacrifice—Rescued Children—Khund Children—Faithfulness of the Converts—Letter from one of them—Miss Packer's Work—The Orphan of Juggernaut, ... 15

CHAPTER III.
INDIA—MADRAS PRESIDENCY.

Early Missions—First Protestant Efforts—Mrs. Mault and the Upper Cloth Riots—Mrs. Anderson—Work in Masulipatam—The Tinivelly Mission—Miss Reade's Work at Punrooty—A Noble Maharani—Palamcottah, ... 72

CHAPTER IV.

INDIA—BOMBAY PRESIDENCY.

Early Missionary Efforts—Mdlle. Janot, Miss Burton, and Mrs. Willing—Mrs. Mullens's Work—Letter from Mrs. Farrar at Nasik—Dr. Wilson's Schools—Bible-women in Bombay—The Indirect Results of Missionary Labour, ... 39

CHAPTER V.

ZENANA MISSIONS.

Meaning of word Zenana—The numerous Societies for carrying on this Work—The Life of a Hindu Married Woman—Native Accounts of their sad State—"Hindu Woman's Prayer"—"Hindu Widows, by one of Themselves"—Difficulties of the Early Workers—Miss Margot—Dr. Duff's Testimony—Gradual Improvement in the Hindu Women—Infanticide—A Zenana Tragedy, . 51

CHAPTER VI.

BATAVIA AND BORNEO.

The first Lady Missionary sent out by the Society for Promoting Female Education in the East—Her Work in Batavia—Mdlle. Combe—Her Removal to Borneo—Conditions under which the Lady Missionaries were sent out, ... 70

CHAPTER VII.

SINGAPORE.

Founding of the Singapore Mission—Miss Grant—Details of her Work—Letter from Hancô—Narratives of Conversions—Miss Cooke—Work sent out for Sale—Mrs. Murray Mitchell's Testimony, ... 79

CHAPTER VIII.

EGYPT.

Miss Holliday and Miss Rogers—Work begun—Request to undertake the Education of the Ladies of the Harem—Miss Holliday's Narrative—Mrs. Leider's Illness—Miss Mary Whately's Schools in Cairo, ... 91

CHAPTER IX.
CHINA.

Early Difficulties—Miss Barker—Miss Aldersey at Ningpo—Story of Ati and Kit—Miss Aldersey's Journals and Letters Story of San Avong—Present State of Female Missions n China, . . . 107

CHAPTER X.
BURMAH.

This Mission begun by American Ladies—Mrs. Judson at Rangoon and Ava—Mrs. Boardman and others at Tavoy—"Six Men for Arracan"—Mrs. Mason and the Karen Mission—Annexation of British Burmah—The Second Mrs. Mason - Her Accounts of the Work among the Karens—Eurasian Girls, ... 121

CHAPTER XI.
PERSIA.

Work of Fidelia Fiske—Incidents in her Labours—Native Converts—Miss Rice—Native Missionaries—Present State of the Work, . 142

CHAPTER XII.
SYRIA, PALESTINE, AND VARIOUS MISSIONS.

Female Missions: Turkey, Greece, and Asia Minor—Mrs. Watson's Work at Lebanon—Jaffa and Beyrout—Mrs. Zeller at Nazareth—The New Orphanage—Mrs. Mungo Ponton's account of Miss Dickson's Work—The Moravians, ... 152

CHAPTER XIII.
FEMALE MEDICAL MISSIONS.

The Story of the Women's Hospital in Bareilly — Mrs. Thomas, Mrs. Parker, and Miss Swain—Gift of the Site—Daily Practice—Miss Monelle and the Wife of the Nawab—Miss Lore, Moradabad—Miss Beilby and the Maharani—Miss Beilby's Visit to England—The Queen's Interest in the Work—Conclusion, ... 167

OUR EASTERN SISTERS

AND

THEIR MISSIONARY HELPERS.

CHAPTER I.

INDIA—BENGAL PRESIDENCY.

" Bring My sons from far, and My daughters from the ends of the earth."—ISAIAH xliii. 6.

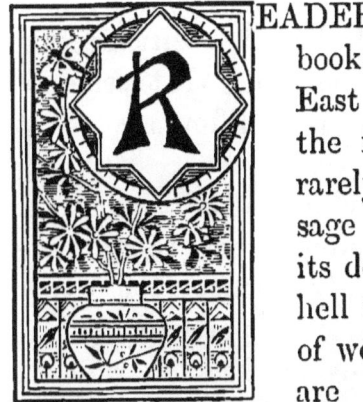READERS of the early reports and books upon mission work in the East must have been struck with the fact that the word " woman " rarely or never occurs. An Eastern sage says : " It is singular that in its descriptions of both heaven and hell the Koran makes no mention of women. The houris of Paradise are creatures of quite another species. The philanthropists and Christians of early days made the same omission. They seem to have forgotten that half the population of the world consisted of women.

The Shasters declare that women have no souls, and for generations English Christians seemed to endorse their statement.

B

In the Shasters Buddha says, "One may trust a tiger come for prey; a thief; a murderer; a savage; even deadly poison, but not a woman."

Menu, the heathen lawgiver, says, "Day and night must a woman be kept in a state of dependence. Though devoid of all good qualities, a husband must be revered by his wife as a god."

A well-known Eastern proverb is, "Cursed be the day that a woman is born."

Some of the best-informed writers on India tell us that it is since the Mohammedan conquest of that country that the women have been so degraded; that previously they were in a much higher position; that there were some learned women; and that some of their earlier sacred books speak very differently about them.

In the early visits paid by missionary ladies in Bengal to native families, nothing struck them more than the misery caused, especially amongst the upper and middle classes, by the practice of polygamy.

They were told that the custom had its origin in the belief constantly taught by the Brahmins that it was only through her husband that any woman could ever reach heaven. The well-known missionary, Ward, in his work, says: "Numbers of the Koolan Brahmins procure a subsistence by polygamy. At their marriages they obtain large dowries, and in their case the girls are allowed to live after marriage in their father's houses. Having married into forty or fifty families, a Koolan goes from house to house, and is there fed, clothed, and lodged. Thus a Hindu possessing only a shred of cloth and his poita (sacred thread) will have more than a hundred wives. The fathers will make any sacrifice to marry their daughters to these Koolan Brahmins, believing that thereby the eternal happiness of the wife is secured. Instances have been known in which Koolans have, although possessed already of scores of wives in different places, married yet more in their dying hours, thereby, as they taught, conferring on the poor deceived women the right to enter heaven."

The Abbé Du Bois says: "The husband may divorce his wife at pleasure, and turn her out of his house, but neither sale nor desertion can release her from her subjection to him."

"Every one who has associated with natives of the East knows that to ask a man about the health of his wife or any female of his household, however ill, or even if dying, would be regarded as a gross insult."

In a certain station the wife of an English official had twin sons. She was on friendly terms with the family of a neighbouring rajah, and on meeting them afterwards, her native friends were loud in their congratulations. One of his wives warmly exclaimed: "How happy should I be if thus blessed!" "But," rejoined the English lady, "what if they had been twin daughters?" "Oh," was the prompt reply, "in that case we should have had them strangled."

A kind-hearted officer, well versed in the language, once tried to comfort a poor, broken-hearted heathen mother as she knelt by the grave of her only son. "Don't talk to her," exclaimed her husband, "she can't understand; she is only a beast." For centuries woman has been regarded by the rich man as a toy to minister to his pleasure, and by the poor man as a slave to supply his wants.

In the following pages we shall record the testimony of natives of both sexes to this state of degradation; but perhaps the fullest published account is in the able work of Shib Chunder Bose, to which we would refer our readers. This gentleman was in the Government service till he resigned his post for the noble life of a missionary. His book was published in London and Calcutta in 1881. He says the miseries of Hindu women literally "beggar description," and adds, "The benevolent exertions of Baboo Keshub Chunder, the Hindu reformer, to promote widow remarriage and female emancipation in general, have not met with the measure of success which they deserve, simply because Hindu society is not ripe for the innovation."

Years passed after the first missionaries went to the East, without any effort being put forth to reach the women. Schwartz was one of those first enlightened on this important subject, and from his life we learn that he established an orphanage at his own cost, and that twelve girls came to be taught with the boys. But he died in 1798, and nothing further was then attempted.

Years rolled by, and zealous and able men left their native land, and lived, and laboured, and died, lamenting that they had seen so few converts, so little fruit. Boys' schools had become numerous, but hopeful scholars, under the influence of heathen mothers, degenerated into idol worshippers. Here and there a noble missionary's wife gathered a few female children around her, and formed the nucleus of a school. Amongst these the names of Mrs. Mault and Mrs. Gogerly rank the first. But removal, ill-health, or death soon scattered their infant gatherings. About 1820 native schools were established by Mrs. Pearce, Mrs. Mundy, Mrs. Mullens, and a few others, and soon after Miss Cooke, better known as Mrs. Wilson, landed in Calcutta, with the avowed object of devoting her life to native female education.

Before proceeding to give details of the early work of these ladies, it may be well to contrast the past with the present, both in India and China. The very name of India excites interest, from whatever point of view it is contemplated. To the Christian women of enlightened countries the condition of millions of their heathen sisters cannot be a matter of indifference. And yet for about two hundred years after the grant of Queen Elizabeth's charter [1] establishing the factories of the East India Company in that land, not one effort had been made for their benefit.

In a most interesting book entitled, "The Pioneers of the Bengal Mission," we have a detailed account of the early work in that presidency from the pen of the last survivor, the Rev. G. Gogerly. He reached India on the 22nd August, 1819, and was informed that

[1] It was in 1599 that a small company of British merchants obtained that charter, and established themselves near a humble fishing village on the Hooghly, about one hundred miles above the mouth of the Ganges. The place was called Kalee Ghaut, or, the landing-place of the goddess Kalee, the tutelary deity of the Thugs. From this is derived the present name of the mighty city of Calcutta.

Government looked upon the introduction of missionaries "as a most dangerous experiment." "We found," he adds, " amongst the Hindus, indifference; amongst the Mohammedans, hatred." He and his fellow-labourers were not, like their predecessors, expelled the country, and for this they were thankful. It was as early as 1793 that William Carey, "the immortal cobbler, who resolved to give to the millions of Hindus the Bible in their own language," landed in Calcutta. When he began his labours on the banks of the Ganges, he was peremptorily ordered by the East Indian Government to desist, or he would at once be sent out of the country. This was no idle threat. Compelled thus to leave his post, he retired to the colony of Serampore, where, all honour to the Danes, he was permitted to commence and carry on his wonderful labours. In Mr. Marshman's touching work, "The Story of Carey, Marshman, and Ward," he says: "These missionaries never considered themselves in any other light than as the pioneers of Christianity in Bengal."

Mrs. Marshman was the first of these labourers to collect the girls in her bungalow, and she in time established several schools. But when the work was once begun, it became obvious to all interested in it, that it was far too vast to be left wholly to the wives of missionaries. Two native schools had been opened in Calcutta in 1820, before the arrival of the first single English lady, Miss Cooke. One of these schools was commenced by Mrs. Pearce, the other by Mrs. Gogerly. "But," writes the husband of the latter lady, "the difficulties they had to encounter almost drove them to despair. The parents declared that the girls must be fetched to and fro, or they would be kidnapped on the way. To remove this fear, Hindu women were paid to go from house to house to fetch them, and then to convey them safely home when school was over."

The next difficulty urged was want of clothing. It was ascertained that a saree costing from one shilling to eighteen pence would make a girl a decent and respectable dress. Kind friends in England purchased these garments, and then the mothers complained that they were losing the benefit of their children's labour in collecting fuel. Anxious to do away with every cause of complaint, it was resolved that one pice (about a farthing and a-half) should be given to every girl who attended school regularly. But even then the attendance was so irregular, that in 1821 Miss Cooke gave up the bazaar schools she had established, and Mrs. Campbell did the same at one she had opened near Kidderpore.

In 1822, Mrs. Gogerly and a missionary friend, through the influence of the late Rammohun Ray, received her first invitation to visit a zenana. It belonged to one of the most powerful noblemen in Calcutta. They were conducted into the ladies' apartments by the young rajah himself. What the ladies saw and heard increased their desire to impart to these suffering sisters the consolations of the Gospel.

A Bengalee newspaper, under date August, 1825, published the following account : " Ramchandra Metha, residing in Calcutta, being attacked by cholera, was taken home by his relatives, and on the night of the 25th died, aged twenty-five. His young and beautiful widow, only about fourteen years of age, thinking herself altogether worthless in the world on the death of her husband, and anticipating the many distresses she would have to suffer if she survived him, absolutely *burnt herself* on the funeral pile." The same paper adds: " Another widow, a little girl of twelve years, obstinately burnt herself on the funeral pile."

Such, or similar horrid rites were actually witnessed by some of these early missionaries. The suttee was abolished by Lord William Bentinck in 1830, but, as some of the native women said, "only leaving them alive to endure one prolonged martyrdom."

It was with such surroundings that the young wives of the pioneer missionaries were combating daily difficulties, when, in the midst of her labour, one was called to her rest. Mr. Gogerly's account of his beloved Mary's last days is most touching. He says that the only house they could obtain consisted of two rooms and a hall upstairs, and the same below, all so damp that it was at the risk of their lives that they slept in them. One was used as a storeroom for materials connected with the press, while the hall was the depository of the Tract Society. "The rain continually falling through the flat roof, we were both prostrated with fever, and my poor wife for nearly a month was delirious, while I was unable to leave my couch. But there was no other place to go to. One day the governor of the jail, a good man, called to see us; and finding we were literally dying for want of better lodgings, kindly offered to convey us to the jail, where he placed two dry rooms at our disposal. We gratefully accepted his offer. But though my dear wife rallied for a time, she gradually became weaker. Our eldest child was at the house of a friend (while I myself had no less than sixty-one boils on my person), when the native servants saw that my dear one was sinking. Overcome by their superstitious fear of death, they all fled, and I was left alone without an individual to take a message or call in a friend. The stillness of death which reigned was only broken by the howling of the jackals and barking of the pariah dogs. It was the dead of night. The baby slept. My wife was still alive, but in a state of coma. I knelt down by the bed-side and audibly commended her spirit to God, when, to my surprise, she raised herself in the bed, and began to pour out her soul in prayer to God in a strain so sweet that it seemed to be a supernatural aid graciously afforded her while passing through the dark valley, enabling her to hold communion with her Father in heaven. She then, without a pang or sigh, gently breathed her last."

Thus on the 12th of September, 1823, being only twenty-four years of age, this sainted labourer entered into rest.

But the fruit of her labours remained. Some of the girls she trained became the wives and mothers of native Christians and teachers. On one occasion several officials in the civil and military service, together with the sister and two daughters of the then acting Governor-General of India, assembled in a native church connected with Mr. Gogerly's mission, numbering two hundred Christian men and women, to witness the baptism of twelve new converts. On that occasion a Brahmin, named Narapot Singh, who had given up an estate worth £30,000 on becoming a Christian, then himself a missionary, took part in the service.

The arrival of Miss Cooke in 1821 as a missionary to the women and children of Calcutta was an event too singular to be lightly regarded, even by the many who care not for such things. She was received by some with scorn and derision, by others with coldness and contempt. Even those who were kind to her advised her at once to secure a return passage in the vessel that brought her out. Intelligent people spoke of her "fool's errand," and doubts were expressed as to her perfect sanity.

Nothing daunted, and aided by the prayers and good wishes of the few who sympathised with her, she at once began studying the Bengalee language. In order to observe the pronunciation, she asked leave to visit a boys' school. Unaccustomed to see a European female in that part of the native town, a crowd collected round the door. Amongst them, with an earnest, wistful look, stood a little unclothed girl, weeping as if her heart would break.

The pundit saw her at the entrance, and coming out drove her away. Miss Cooke requested her interpreter to call the child, when the pundit said that she had been for three whole months begging him to teach her with the boys. Laying her hands upon the little bare shoulder, Miss Cooke gently asked: "Little girl, why do you cry so? Tell me." Frightened at being addressed by a white lady, the child would have fled. But Miss Cooke lovingly repeated the question. Amid her sobs, the little one faltered : " I want to go to the school! I want to be taught! But—I am *only* a girl." Promising the weeping child that her wish should be gratified, the astonished pundit said, that if the lady really liked to teach her, he would bring twenty more the very next day.

This effort was crowned with abundant success. Within a single month two girls' schools were established, and ere long between 200 and 300 were in daily attendance. For many years Mrs. Wilson's " Central School" and "The Orphan Asylum at Agrapara," in the suburbs, have been as household words in the city of Calcutta.

The next unmarried labourer who began this work of faith and labour of love was Miss Bird, who left for India in 1823. The different missionary societies were now by their publications diffusing intelligence and arousing interest, while Mrs. Sherwood's " Henry and his Bearer," and other little books on India, were awakening curiosity in the minds of hundreds of children in Christian households.

Miss Bird was induced at first, by the affection she bore to her widowed brother in India, to leave her home to comfort him in his sorrow. He was occupying an important post in the Civil Service at Gorruckpore, and at once yielded to her earnest desire to make some efforts for the degraded women by whom she was surrounded.

After some years of daily toil in that city she removed to Calcutta. Her knowledge of the language was now so perfect that she resolved to devote her fortune and her life to those who, speaking only

Hindustani, were unable to benefit by instruction in English, or to read any language at all. Nor was this all; for she translated many valuable books into that language, and wrote in it a Commentary on Genesis; an Outline of Ancient History; a Treatise on Astronomy, and other tracts and school books. In addition to daily religious instruction to the girls, she established a Sunday-school and Bible-classes for the women. So remarkable was her method of communicating knowledge, that she was requested by several ladies conducting boarding-schools for the daughters of officers and civilians to devote some time each week to giving religious instruction to their pupils.

In the midst of these abounding labours she was suddenly called to her rest. The night before her death she passed at the Kidderpore Orphanage, telling the little ones of the love of Jesus. About half-past six in the morning she became so ill that a dear lady friend, and her valued pastor, Archdeacon Corrie, were sent for. She whispered that, like Moses, she could wish to remain for the sake of her poor people. A short time before, when advised to return home on furlough, she said: "I cannot think of it while I have such a field of labour, and, undeserving as I am, such refreshings from on High." After a few hours' illness, she gently slept in Jesus.

In 1824 a Ladies' Society for Native Female Education was formed in Calcutta, which had, for a time, a branch association in London; but that branch soon became extinct, and for some years no distinct organisation for the benefit of heathen women existed in Great Britain. Meanwhile, our American sisters had been more active, and had sent workers into the mission field on several stations. A pamphlet called "Articles of the Boston Female Society for Missionary Purposes," tells of its formation in 1800; and nineteen years afterwards "The Female Missionary Society of the American Methodist Episcopal Church" was formed, and there are now no less than twenty women's missionary societies in that land.

The year 1834 was a remarkable one in the annals of British female missions. The well known and highly honoured American missionary to China, the Rev. David Abeel, had broken down in the midst of his toil, and had come to England to rest and recruit his strength, before he returned to die. But his heart was so full of the sorrows of heathen women that he could not be silent. Wherever he went, their degradation, and the duties of Christian women at home towards them, was his one theme. He impressed upon the committees of the different societies that the whole apparatus of missionary effort must be deficient if not met by a distinct and appropriate machinery for the enlightenment and conversion of the women. He drew up and printed a powerful appeal to the Christian women of Great Britain and America. As a result, a number of ladies formed themselves into a committee, and "The Society for Promoting Female Education in China, India, and the East" was established. Four years later this title was abridged to its present name, "The Society for Promoting Female Education in the East."

The first meeting was held under the auspices of the Honourable and Rev. Baptist W. Noel, in the vestry of St. John's Chapel, Bedford Row, London.

A working committee consisting of twenty-four ladies of different Christian denominations was formed. The small committee in London previously referred to in connection with the Calcutta Society, having become extinct, its treasurer, and only remaining member, Mrs. Hugh Hill, joined the newly formed society, paying over to the treasurer the small sum of £12 remaining in her hands, the committee having determined on sending a helper to Mrs. Wilson's school in Calcutta. Miss Wakefield, the lady thus appointed, was the second sent out. Of Miss Thornton, the first agent, we shall hear more as our narrative proceeds. She went to Batavia. The above is a short account of the commencement of female schools in Bengal. The success attending them paved the way for more extended efforts, which are now being carried on for the same object by all the missionary societies, and many isolated workers.

As indicating the growth of the work in Calcutta the following statistics have just been published :—

Pupils in Schools and Zenanas—

Church of Scotland,	1418
American,	1169
Society for Propagation of the Gospel,	542
London Mission,	491
Baptist Mission,	440
Free Church Mission,	368
TOTAL,	4428

CHAPTER II.

INDIA.—ORISSA.

"The dark places of the earth are full of the habitations of cruelty."
PSALMS lxxiv. 20.

PERHAPS few parts of India are less known to English readers than Berhampore and Cuttack, in the large province of Orissa. The wives of two missionaries connected with the General Baptist Society, applied in 1840 to the Female Education Society for a lady to help them. Theirs was the only agency at work in that part of the world, and their schools were established mainly for the benefit of the people called Khunds or Khoonds. The Society sent out Miss Derry, Miss Poppy, Miss Packer, and others. How admirably these ladies have carried out their work will be shown by the fact, that in 1881, besides the number of girls in the two orphanages, there were in the village schools around Cuttack 1349 children being taught the pure Word of God. It is a singular fact, that at the present time these three ladies are still engaged in missionary work.

Through the kindness of Mrs. Buckley (formerly Miss Derry), the only member still resident in India of the party who left England in 1843, we are furnished with the following account: "Khondistan, where the Khoonds live, is a country little known, and the name of the race does not appear in some of our geographies. Their history is not written in any of our annals. Seventy years ago the country was altogether unexplored. The district in which Government operations have been conducted extends from 19° 30′ to 20° 50′ north latitude, and from 83° 40′ to 84° 50′ east longitude. In the district thus comprised, for many a dreary century deeds of surpassing cruelty have been perpetrated. War has often been overruled by God to accomplish His wise and holy designs. It was in this way the atrocities of Khondistan were disclosed to the civilised world. In 1836 an insurrection broke out in Goomsur, in which the Khoonds were implicated. Troops were sent to quell the rebellion, and while so engaged, it was discovered that human beings were immolated on the altar of a sanguinary superstition. This was called the Meriah sacrifice, the victim being designated a Meriah. Female infanticide was also practised. The rites are perfectly distinct. One is a public sacrifice of a victim of full age, who has been fattened for the slaughter; the other the murder of a new-born girl. The Government agents endeavoured to obtain a registry of the men, their wives, and the number of children; but the people fled in terrible alarm, declaring that if numbered they were all sure to die.

The Meriah rite is not a propitiation for sin, but an offering to the Earth Goddess, whose malignity they dread, and whom they hope in this way to propitiate, that they may obtain plentiful crops. There is no identity between the Kalee of the Hindus and this Earth Goddess of the Khunds. A gentleman well acquainted with the people and their customs says, that the sacrifice would be of no avail unless the victim was bought with a price. The people from twelve to fifteen miles round are thus yearly gathered together in the places where the sacrifice is to be offered. There is music, and dancing, and beating of drums, and a kind of Highland pipe. Some of our dear rescued children have sung us the song which precedes the horrible rite. It is as follows :—

> " Hail, Mother, hail ! Hail, Goddess Bhobanee !
> Lo ! we present a sacrifice to thee;
> Partake thereof, and let it pleasure give,
> And in return let us thy grace receive.
> In all our fields, and all the plots we sow,
> Oh, let a rich and plenteous harvest grow."

The victim, often a young girl, is bound, food offered, with the reminder that soon there will be no power to take more. On being bound to a tree, the signal is given ; the jani, or chief priest, commences the horrid slaughter ; the maddened crowd, all armed with sharp knives, rush on, and cut the flesh from the bones ! The flesh is then deposited in the fields to ensure a plentiful crop. Two or three days pass, and the same scene is witnessed in another, and yet another village, so that one person may see ten or twelve of these murders in a single season.

From the time these dreadful disclosures were made the Indian Government has used means to suppress the inhuman rites. A Christian officer, a captain in the Madras army, had the honour of rescuing the first twelve children in 1837. They were placed in the mission school at Berhampore, near Ganjam, and some have run their earthly race, but not till they knew a Saviour's love, and felt its transforming power in their hearts. One of this number when dying said: "I love the Lord, and know He will not leave me. I am a great sinner, but Christ died to save sinners." On the night she died, many of her school companions sat with her, and at her request sang hymns. Just before she expired she said: "Sing Hallelujah! I am going home." For several years these rescued children had no support from Government. Some *were given* by the authorities to the missionaries, and some to Hindus, Mohammedans, and Portuguese. But in 1847 a change in the officials led to their being taken by Government, placed in the mission schools, and taught a trade or farming. The girls were generally married at sixteen. In two years, no less than 547 victims were thus rescued.

An officer, himself an able linguist, reduced the language to a written character, and, aided by the missionaries, a mission press was set up, and books prepared and printed in the Khund language.

Since this was effected Nagpore has been annexed to the British territories, and a good road through Goomsur and Boad to Sohnpore made, which, in a commercial point of view, is a great boon, as it facilitates the sale of the salt manufactured in the Ganjam district. Thus the Gospel has again been proved to have the promise of "the life that now is, as well as of that which is to come."

Another missionary lady writes, August, 1848: "The other day, while giving my pupils a lesson in geography, a messenger came saying, 'Fifty Khund children have come.' We gave them a hearty welcome, but they were wild and uncultivated in the extreme;—their hair long and uncombed; their dress a piece of coarse native calico wrapped round the waist, with one end brought over the shoulders. They had not been taught a single useful art, but had spent their time in idleness, or gathering wild fruits and roots. Our first business was to get them a thorough bath; we then had their hair cut. In the interim of school hours I cut out a complete set of new clothes, consisting of a coloured petticoat and striped jacket, with short sleeves for each. Miss Collins thus describes an affecting recognition: 'One of my former Khund children, a sweet girl of ten, named Berdomie, had retained her own language better than the others. She manifested much solicitude for her new friends, going from one to another, and comforting any that wept. They were very anxious to see the boys, and find their brothers. Some of them were taken over to the compound and did find them, the strong likeness bearing testimony to the fact, when they laid their hands on their heads and wept much.'"

Another lady writes: "Six more of our dear Meriah girls are now happily married. It makes our hearts thrill with gratitude when we think that had not kind hands been stretched out for their rescue they would long ere this have been immolated in the cause of vile idolatry. Another dear girl, apparently about eleven, bids fair to rival all the others. She works beautifully, and is so quick and clever. She was just on the point of being sacrificed when rescued, the first cut having been made in her leg, the mark of which she will carry with her to her grave. Our assistant teacher, a pious intelligent young widow, is also a rescued Khund.

"The girls have been reading 'Daybreak in Britain,' and the similarity between what is there described and their own superstitions struck them much." I Kide, this teacher, was rescued by Captain Fry a few weeks before the time appointed for the sacrifice. She had seen many, and her parents told her that she would one day be offered up in the same way. She minutely described the awful tragedy of the last sacrifice she witnessed. Then she too was sold, fastened up, and prepared by being fattened. She was dreadfully frightened and tried to make her escape, when they fastened her with large chains round her ankles, to make it impossible. But the time of her deliverance was at hand. The brave, kind-hearted officer heard of the coming sacrifice, and rode night and day to save her. He succeeded, placed her in the mission school, where her heart and intellect were cultivated, and now she is an earnest, intelligent Christian woman, training others for heaven. Oole, another dear rescued one, is suffering severely in her eyes. It appears that often before the rite begins, the victim is rendered almost senseless in various ways. Amongst others, a mixture of oil and other ingredients is thrown over the head and face. It blinds them for the time. This was done to poor Oole, and she has never recovered; but I hope the dear girl is a child of God, and though so suffering she is rejoicing in a sense of His favour and forgiveness. When I asked her what led to the change, she said 'that one night she sat thinking of the great deliverance God had effected for *her body;* this led her to seek a still greater deliverance for her soul.'"

The decision of these young converts was remarkable, and, as their numbers increased, attracted much attention. The wicked were emboldened in their wickedness, and sought to lay snares for them. One day a roll of paper was found tied up in the compound addressed to them. The writer described himself as in Government employ, receiving a good salary; and they were told that if any of them would secretly leave the premises, which they were well able to do, a place was named for meeting, and they should at once be placed in a position which should enable them to wear the finest garments and jewellery. "What is your present position?" the letter went on to say. "You are just the slaves of the missionaries. You know no joys, wear coarse garments;" and much more in the same strain. What was the result of that letter? To God be all the glory. The Bible truths had so enlightened the minds of our dear children that these specious statements took no effect. Bringing the letter to their beloved friend and teacher, one of the elder girls as spokeswoman said: "We know the pleasures of sin are only for a season, followed by shame, remorse, death, and endless woe."

As workers increased, schools and a large orphan asylum were established. In the latter, one of the number, little Violet, was soon called to her heavenly rest. When near her end she said: "Do not give me more medicine, I shall not recover; God is calling me to go above. I am not afraid to die; Jesus has died for me, and I know my sins are all forgiven."

"The history of one little girl resembles that of many others. Her parents were on a pilgrimage to Juggernaut, when the mother was seized with cholera. Her cruel husband left her; when overcome with disease and exhaustion, she lay down and died. Next morning she was found with her baby lying at her breast. The heart of a native Christian woman was touched with compassion. She adopted the babe, gave it the name of Rebecca, and placed her at our school. She is now an intelligent child, and reads the Bible nicely."

Later on, it was the privilege of these ladies to begin work in the homes of the high-born natives. An educated babu, employed as inspector of Government boys' schools, had taught his wife to read in her own tongue. He invited the English ladies to visit her. Several friends came in, and sat round on a newly-spread carpet. They listened attentively to the hymns sung and the old, old story of Jesus and His love.

When obliged to go, several exclaimed: "Oh, do come again quickly;" and great was the thankfulness with which on a later visit they found that the Bible was being read diligently. This was in Pooree, a place noted for idolatry.

We add part of a letter written in English by one of the young converts, after her marriage to a native teacher residing at Balasore. It is addressed to her former schoolfellows.

"My beloved sisters, with loving salutations I write you a little letter. I had trouble in body and mind on my long journey. Being unaccustomed to riding, the shaking of the cart made me very sick. I was constantly thinking about you all. When I saw beautiful flowers, I wanted you to see them. If I fell asleep in my dreams, I was with you, and thought myself in your midst, singing the hymns we have so often sung. Then I awoke and found myself far away, not one of you near me; but at length I gained comfort by casting my burden upon the Lord. The Christian sisters are very kind to me, but I cannot yet love them as I do you. Let us pray for one another. — Your loving sister, LOUISA."

Miss Packer is still diligently carrying on her work in Orissa, after twenty-six years of faithful labour. There are now 180 inmates of the female orphanage under the care of Miss Leigh. Very many others of the girls scattered through the province are practically exhibiting in their Christian homes the benefit of the instruction they have received.

The report of the Orissa Mission for 1881-1882

states that, in addition to a larger distribution of the Word of God than in previous years, there have been many additions to their literature in the vernacular. The "Pilgrim's Progress," a work on fulfilled prophecy, and many others of general interest, have been translated into Oriya. In Dr. Hunter's "Imperial Gazetteer of India" we find this interesting notice: "Choga, or Chagan Gobra, a village of Orissa, inhabited *exclusively* by a small community of peasant Christians, and two other Christian hamlets adjoin it." It is worthy of notice, that while in the part still heathen, the examiners report that only *one woman in nineteen hundred* is able to read and write; in some of the Christian villages, out of 175 females, 87, or about half, are able to do so. It adds: "This proves that the girls' school, supported by the Female Education Society, has done a good work."

One little romance, in connection with our sisters in Orissa, must close this chapter. As far ago as 1829, a Brahmin pundit from North India set out with his wife and their only surviving child, then a few months old, on a pilgrimage to the temple of Juggernaut. Though a girl she was loved, and week after week the mother carried her little one uncomplainingly under the burning sun, toward the holy shrine.

When within a few miles of the temple, the parents were attacked with cholera. The man died, and Dr. Sutton, a devoted missionary, passing by to preach to the pilgrims, found the mother lying on the ground, and her starving infant clinging to her. Alone, with a fearful storm raging around him, the missionary could only lift up his heart for guidance. He walked some miles before he could procure milk or medicine; but when administered, the poor creature rallied. For three days she lingered, and listened for the first time in her life to the story of a Saviour's love. Then by signs commending her little one to the Good Samaritan who had done so much for her, she expired. What was to be done with the baby? It was a girl. No heathen woman could be induced to tend it. The native doctor whom Mrs. Sutton had called in shrugged his shoulders, saying, "Let it die too. What else?" But this was not to be. While the doctor was taking possession of the bangles and other ornaments on the lifeless body, Dr. and Mrs. Sutton formed the resolution to adopt the Hindu baby. They were childless, and, as years rolled on, the baby grew into a young woman. She had accompanied her adopted parents to America, had been placed in a good school, and become a useful and educated Christian. On her return to Orissa, preserved from the evils of the early marriage of her countrywomen, she undertook the training of the girls connected with the mission. In course of time a young Rajput, who had become a Christian, and had received a liberal education, visited the station. He wooed and won in true English fashion the gentle orphan girl, and with the glad consent of the foster-parents the marriage took place. The union was consecrated by a Christian service, and the presence of Jesus was sought at the wedding feast. The orphan of Juggernaut still lives to bless God for her wonderful preservation, and all the blessings of this life which have been vouchsafed to her. This story was told by her husband, Behari Lal Singh, who concluded his speech by asking his hearers "to pray for his beloved wife," that she may "be a burning and shining light among her benighted sisters, and have wisdom and grace given to train up their children in the nurture and admonition of the Lord."

CHAPTER III.

INDIA—MADRAS PRESIDENCY.

"These are they which came out of great tribulation, and have washed their robes and made them white in the blood of the Lamb."
—REV. vii. 14.

THE first English settlement in this presidency took place when a Hindu rajah presented Cromwell with a small strip of land which was named, after England's patron saint, Fort St. George. Here the agents of the East India Company established themselves.

We have undoubted evidence that the light of the Gospel had penetrated into Southern India from the early ages of Christianity.

When Vasco de Gama landed on the coast of Malabar about the year 1503, he found upwards of a hundred Christian churches. "These churches," said the Portuguese, "belong to the Pope." "Who is the Pope?" replied the natives; "we never even heard of him." Three centuries later Dr. Buchanan, visiting the same country, writes, that as he approached the church of Chinganoor he met one of the Syrian clergy, who saluted him with these words, "The God of peace be with thee." The people "of the neighbouring villages," he adds, "came round me, women as well as men. The sight of women assured me that I was once more in a Christian country, for Hindu and Mohammedan women are accounted by the men as an inferior race, and in general are confined to the house for life, like irrational creatures."

The first Protestant mission to South India was founded by Ziegenbalg in 1705, in Tanjore. He returned to Europe in 1714; and it is an interesting fact that one of the first letters written by King George the First, after coming to the British throne, was to this missionary. His Majesty honoured Ziegenbalg with an audience, and expressed his deep interest in the translation of the Bible into Tamul, which was then progressing.

After the death of Ziegenbalg, the mission, which included schools for girls as well as for boys, was kept up by no less than fifty successive missionaries, including the honoured names of Schultz, Gérické, Schwartz, and Kothoff, and subsequently by Rhenius. At the time of Dr. Buchanan's visit, the Mohammedans had held dominion for many years over a large part of India, and had greatly persecuted these Syrian Christians. Though persecuted, they were not forsaken, and many could testify that the religion of Christ was no cunningly devised fable. Amidst prevailing vice and idolatry, some of these remarkable people are still found, an interesting remnant of Christianity in a heathen land. In some of the congregations which Buchanan addressed, the women occupied one side of the church, neatly clothed in white jackets and light muslin veils.

In 1806, Ringeltaube, a Russian missionary, was sent out at the request of an Englishman, Colonel C. Macaulay, then the Resident at the court of Travancore, who longed to benefit the souls as well as the bodies of the people. Not only did he obtain permission from the rajah for the missionary to settle in his dominions, but he offered himself to defray his expenses. Schools for both sexes were established there, and in other places, by the missionaries of the Society for the Propagation of the Gospel, and under this Resident and his successor, Colonel Monro, who was equally interested in the spread of the Gospel, schools and other Christian work flourished.

In 1819, Mrs. Mault, the wife of a London missionary, brought a large number of girls under instruction, and for thirty-six years laboured in South India. She introduced amongst them the art of lace-making, which proved a great temporal help. For a time this mission prospered, but Satan's kingdom was beginning to be shaken, and he now raised up a fierce persecution. As the whole story is connected with women, it bears directly upon our subject. The outbreak began in 1827, and arose in the following way. It had always been forbidden the Shanars and all other low caste women to wear any clothing whatever above the waist. The truer and better instinct had been aroused by the teaching of Christianity, and the Christian women and girls adopted a plain loose cotton jacket with short sleeves, over their skirts, as devised for them by one of the missionary ladies. This displeased the Súdra aristocracy, and they resolved to use it as an excuse to put an end to Christianity, and its reforms and innovations.

Threats were uttered, several school-houses burned down, and a stop put to others that were being erected. One native gentleman, who had befriended the missionaries, and sold them the ground upon which a mission house and school for girls had been built at Neyoor, was seized, imprisoned on false charges, and not released for seven years. Spies were sent about the country, converts were thrust into dungeons, their Bibles and school-books cast into the roads, while their women were beaten and insulted in the bazaars, and in many cases their clothing was publicly torn off. On the 29th of February, 1829, a proclamation was issued forbidding all low caste women to wear "any upper cloth" whatever, as it was contrary to ancient custom.

Notwithstanding this cruel persecution converts were added to the Church, and some local changes for a time caused a lull, and the storm seemed to have blown over. Notwithstanding efforts by succeeding governors to extend education, the rest was but of short continuance. We learn in a letter from the widow of Sir Robert Grant, that his successor as governor, the young Lord Elphinstone, as one of his first acts, invited a statement of all the educational institutions in India before he introduced reforms into his own province of Madras.

But the people did not seem ripe for the change. The Rev. J. Abbs, in his interesting work entitled "Twenty-two Years in Travancore," states, that in

1858 there were between 10,000 and 11,000 native Christians in the district round Neyoor. Suddenly the "upper cloth riots" again burst forth. A Christian woman was assaulted in the public market and her clothes torn off from her. The Súdras gave out that a fresh order had been issued by Government to strip every Christian low caste woman of her jacket. Such cruelties and outrages were perpetrated that Lord Harris, then Governor of Madras, looked carefully into the matter, and found that reports had been circulated that he had caused a proclamation to be made giving over the rule to the native rajah, with liberty to murder all Europeans. In consequence, many of the Christians had been placed in the stocks, severely beaten, their houses entered, and the women attacked with clubs and knives, their money, goods, and jewels stolen, and themselves cruelly beaten and kicked. Through the effectual interposition of Sir Charles Trevelyan, who succeeded Lord Harris as Governor of Madras, these poor creatures were protected, and their right to wear decent clothing recognised by law.

Sir Charles addressed the resident in the following strong language: "The whole civilised world would cry shame upon us if we did not make a firm stand; and I should fail in respect to Her Majesty, if I attempted to describe the feelings with which she must regard the use made against her own sex of the promises of protection so graciously accorded by her." The special object of the royal proclamation was to assure Her Majesty's Indian subjects of liberty of thought and action, so long as they did not interfere with the just rights of others. As a result of Sir

Charles's act the rajah issued a proclamation in 1859 allowing all his women subjects to wear "a dress of coarse cloth."

From this time the work in South India increased rapidly. Instead, as in former years, of the female scholars belonging exclusively to the low caste classes, education is now eagerly sought by high caste girls and their male relatives. Government has joined in giving it to them as well as to boys. The public prints have even stated that there are already some heathen female schools in India. Nevertheless, woman's education is for the most part still in the hands of the various missionary societies, and it is well that it should be so. What benefits would our poor sisters gain, if, taught by secular knowledge to realise their own past degradation, we did not at the same time give them the bread of life, and lead them to the woman's Saviour?

The record of female missions in Madras would be incomplete without a reference to Mrs. Anderson. In 1846 she left her Swiss home, and for thirteen years devoted all her energies, in connection with the Free Church of Scotland, to work among the women of the Madras presidency. When obliged to seek rest for a time in her native land, an address signed by no less than 200, including Mohammedans, Hindus, and East Indians, was presented to her, with an earnest prayer for her speedy return.

In 1841 the Revs. R. Noble and Henry Fox landed in Madras, and at once proceeded to Masulepatam, the chief town of the Telugu nation. Soon after their arrival Mrs. Fox had work found for her by Mr. Tucker, then the head of the Church Mission. A European died leaving two children. He had married a Telugu woman who had been a dancing girl, and the children had been brought up in heathenism. Mr. Tucker was appointed their guardian, and he entrusted the little wild ignorant girl to the young missionary's wife. She had been thoroughly imbued with heathen superstitions, and it was with difficulty she could be taught to eat with a spoon, sit upon a chair, or wear a decent dress, and it was a long struggle ere she could sit at table where people would *see her eat*. During the time she spent with Mr. and Mrs. Fox a great and saving change took place, and she gave evident signs of having become a true Christian. Mr. Fox writes: "Mary Paterson is more than ever precious to me, as the crown of rejoicing to my dear wife. Only four years ago she was brought to us a heathen wild cat, and now she is such a beautiful Christian character, yearning and striving after the conversion of her heathen relatives."

In "India's Women," Sir Richard Temple states, May, 1881: "There are now no fewer than 70,000 girls at school in British India." On the other hand, in the "Indian Evangelical Review" for July, 1882, it is stated that there are still in the Madras presidency alone 2,800,000 girls still untaught.

The royal visit of the "Heir-apparent" to the throne of Travancore, to different missions and schools, and, amongst others, to Mrs. Bishop's caste girls' school, tended much to wear away the prejudices of the natives. He expressed his appreciation of the training there given, by sending a present of maps and school-books, and won the hearts of all the children by himself giving each little girl a small present.

The late Rev. John Tucker, the superintendent of the Church Missionary Society's missions in Madras, on hearing of the establishment of the Female Education Society, wrote thus to its secretary in 1836 asking for help: "Our great want is teachers—females of moderate talents and attainments, of patient spirit, unambitious, and content to work for the Lord's sake." In response to this appeal four ladies were sent to Mr. Tucker and his sister. Miss Craven was placed at Palamcottah, 400 miles to the south, where the delicate health of both the missionaries' wives prevented them from carrying out the work they had begun. Mrs. Pettitt had twenty-nine girls under instruction, and the numbers soon increased.

The rich blessing which has rested upon the Tinnevelly Mission is known to all interested in missionary work. In addition to the Sarah Tucker institution and the Florence Monro school, supported originally by two ladies in memory of one "gone home," there are boarding, day, orphan, and branch schools. In one opened in the Panneiveli district, an interesting case was that of Rachel, a girl of the "Marraver" or thief caste. She learned to love and fear the God of the Bible, when her father, a very bad man, came to carry her off, and marry her to a heathen. This she refused to do, when her stepmother came and said, if she would not consent she should be murdered. Still Rachel refused. Then her brother and two other heathen men came to take her by force. Friends took up her case and applied to the magistrate, when Rachel begged no one might be punished, but only that she might be protected. She has since become a teacher, and continues to be a humble, consistent Christian.

Writing of this work, the late Bishop of Madras said: "There was a simple reality about the scene before me, which made my heart run over. Would that the opponents of missions could have been present." This, too, is a scene with many a parallel in Tinnevelly. In 1817 the Rev. J. Hough, a devoted chaplain and missionary, recorded two villages from which caste, devil worship, and heathenism were banished. Now their number is nearly 500. The women in these villages may be seen sitting beneath the shade of the cocoa-nut trees spinning their cotton, and singing Tamul hymns, and the children learning their first lessons of Christianity at their mothers' knees.

The Rev. W. Keane wrote to the Female Education Society in 1853: "During the six years I was in India I saw no aspect of the mission field so urgent in its claims, or so promising in its results, as that of native female education. I long to tell your Society of the heavy sufferings of heathen women, and that I have seen in *your* Society *the only* remedy."

In Miss Lowe's interesting work on Punrooty, we have a striking illustration of what two feeble women were enabled to effect, living alone and surrounded by thousands of heathen natives. Many of the Mussulmans of both sexes would come and listen to a white lady, often exclaiming: "If it had been a padre, we would never have come." Punrooty being a purely native town, unreached by any modern or European ideas, the difficulty of gaining access to high caste women was unusually great. When a Brahmin sub-magistrate, who owed his elevation to Miss Reade's father, was asked by her permission to visit his wife, he replied: "We are not sufficiently enlightened for that here." At a house where the favour was granted, one of the family told her: "We are unclean through your coming among us. We shall all have the trouble of bathing when you are gone."

Miss Reade's sympathy with the sorrowful little child-widows revealed to her much of the misery and some of the secrets of a Mohammedan zenana, where it was said: "Many may be murdered and buried without any one outside knowing." In many instances she has been permitted to see the fruit of her labours.

Khadu Bee was married when seven years old to a havildar (non-commissioned officer), and had from that time followed the regiment in a closely-covered cart. On her husband's death she was left penniless. Her own words to Miss Reade were: "When you met me I was losing my senses. It was only God's words of love and peace you spoke that kept me from going mad. When my husband was alive, I had land, cows, and sheep, all I wanted for this world, but no light in my mind. Now I have lost all, but light has come to me." On her baptism, her relatives were told they ought to kill her. Poisoned milk was sent to her, and other attempts made to murder her. She often said: "No one knows the murders that take place in our houses at midnight." One of her own relatives had been murdered by her husband and bricked up in the wall for no other crime than having rushed into the road to save her own child from being knocked down by a bullock cart. Her husband was told she had been seen outside her house. He said little, but after the midnight following no one ever saw her again.

A recent missionary journal records the following story as illustrating the results of a Christian woman's work in South India. In the palace of a maharajah, the royal ladies have been permitted to receive the visits of a lady, sent out by the Church Missionary Society. The husband of one of these princesses had the misfortune to offend his highness the maharajah. He accused his royal relative of disloyalty, and threw him into prison, where he lay for five years. Thus separated from her husband, the rajah commanded the lady to marry another, a man of his choice. For those five long years did that noble woman resist his authority and threats, backed as they were by members of her own family. "No," she said, "he, the captive, was her own lawful husband. She had read the Bible, and must obey God. That book had taught her her duty, and she would die rather than marry another."

At the end of five years the tyrant rajah himself died, and one of the first acts of his successor was to set the prisoner free. The loving and faithful wife was restored to husband and home.

The first female boarding school established by the Church Missionary Society was in Palamcottah, in 1823, and the circumstances which led to it were extremely interesting. Mrs. Schnarré, the energetic young wife of one of the early missionaries, was very anxious to acquire the language. In those days this was not an easy matter. The only intercourse with female natives was confined to those of the lowest caste, from whom the lady felt she was not likely to obtain either grammar or correct pronunciation. She therefore resolved to go regularly to the boy's school, and listen to the pundit's mode of teaching. A little boy, attracted perhaps by the white lady's gentle manner, ventured one day to creep to her side, and beg as a great boon that she would give him a spelling-book. As he had one at school, the request led to further inquiries, when the boy confessed that he wanted the book for his little sister at home, who was longing to read. Further acquaintance with that and similar houses led Mrs. Schnarré to make friends with the mothers. One of them informed her, not only that girls did not need to learn anything beyond what their mothers taught them, but that all girls' learning was comprised in three things. First, to keep caste; secondly, to make salaam; and thirdly, how to deceive. She often afterwards heard them boast how many clever falsehoods their girls could tell.

God's blessing has rested upon the work of His handmaidens. Educated native gentlemen in India, and especially in Madras, are now trying to secure the blessings of education and freedom of choice in marriage for their sisters and daughters. Quite lately, at the annual distribution of prizes at a Madras girls' school, in connection with the London Missionary Society, a Hindu gentleman presided, and stated that he was not over-rating the importance of female education, when he said that it was one of the most powerful agents in the progress of the country, though it had not entered yet beyond the stage of its infancy.

CHAPTER IV.

INDIA—BOMBAY PRESIDENCY.

"I commend unto you Phebe, our sister, for she hath been a succourer of many."—ROMANS xvi. 1, 2.

FROM the report on Education in British India, made by the Government of India in 1872 to the Home Department, we learn that the first educational experiments in Bombay were some charity schools opened in 1718. In them white and coloured children were dependent upon public benevolence until the Company, in 1807, made a grant for educational purposes. In the charter of 1813, when Parliament gave India its first bishop and chaplains, a department was formed for public instruction. In 1815 the Bombay Native Education Society was formed, under the auspices of its governor, Mountstuart Elphinstone. So little were these efforts appreciated, that when the Rev. Dr. Wilson, the well-known Scotch missionary, made his first tour in 1829, an entry in his journal, under date

13th November in that year, states that twenty-four boys and one solitary girl were among the most hopeful results.

The American missionaries were the first in the field, and in 1810 took up the work which in early Christian centuries the Nestorians had begun. Dr. Carey, at his Serampore press, had translated the whole of the New Testament into Marathee, the spoken language of Bombay, so that the Americans, then the London Missionary Society in 1815, and the Church missionaries afterwards, had it ready to hand.

Dr. Murray Mitchell states that he and Wilson and other Scotch missionaries wished to settle in and open schools at Poona and other large cities, as they considered Bombay was already cared for. But a high official told them that "the authorities were so desperately afraid of offending the Brahmins that this could not be permitted." Under these circumstances, Dr. Wilson and his young wife began their labours in Bombay. She felt deeply interested in the welfare of the heathen females, and at once established three girls' schools. The Christian public took up this work, many details of which were published by Mrs. Wilson in the "Oriental Christian Spectator." Her labours were cut short by her early death, but in the very year that she died she was able to rejoice at the gift of the ladies of Bombay, who subscribed 700 rupees to aid the object so near her heart. To the end she cared for her poor Marathi girls, and calling one of them to her she exclaimed: "Oh, Anandie, I beseech you greatly, love Jesus Christ. The prospect of death is sweet." Shortly after her death, the eldest girl in her school was united in marriage to a Brahmin convert. It was the first Christian native wedding in Bombay.

In 1833, Archdeacon Carr was made first Bishop of Bombay, and from that time the work of female education received a new impetus.

Hearing of the newly formed Society for Promoting Female Education, he wrote to the secretary as follows: "In consequence of information communicated to me of the readiness of the Society to render help in selecting and sending out to India ladies to undertake the management of female schools, I am induced earnestly to solicit their aid in procuring a suitable mistress for a school lately opened at Poona. We are, in this presidency, commencing the education of native females. I may say without hesitation that there is no likelihood of finding a suitable person in India."

To meet this application, a lady was at once sent out, and soon after, at the request of the missionaries connected with the General Assembly of the Church of Scotland, Mdlle. Jallot, a French Protestant lady supported by the Scottish Ladies' Association, followed, and began work in Bombay. Mdlle. Jallott was a convert from Romanism, and had literally given up all for Christ. She entered upon her work with a heart full of love to souls, and talents of no common order. But her career was soon ended. "She was seized with cholera in so severe a form" that, as wrote the Rev. Robert Nesbit, "it hurried away the powers of body and mind." In a lucid interval, looking lovingly at the friends who surrounded her bed, she exclaimed: "I am not afraid to die!" And her bright smile when speechless told how she fed upon the texts they repeated. "You are," he adds, "highly favoured in having helped forward such a saint. You have blessed the heathen by setting before them a bright example of the power of the Gospel, and the very words which in her incipient labours were uttered and re-uttered in a stammering tongue may become the seed of spiritual life."

God's work was not hindered. Other workers came forward, and the next year Miss Burton and Mrs. Willing arrived in Bombay. The former filled the vacant post, while the latter took charge of the military asylum, at which place, and afterwards in other parts of India, she faithfully laboured for twenty years. The first-fruits soon began to appear. Two women were baptised. The first was a Marathi widow. One day when her teacher was praying with her, tears rolled from her eyes, as she exclaimed: "I was thinking what a sinful girl I was." The other said: "I know that I am a sinner, and that Christ alone can take away my sins. I do wish to be a Christian, because I want all my sins to be forgiven, I want a clean heart." Afterwards she said: "God does not find in us good hearts that want just a little of His help, but He sees that we want quite new hearts, which He only can create. I am a sinful child. I cannot save myself, but Jesus Christ can make my heart good." Two days after her baptism she was married to an excellent native catechist from Nagpore. He had made a journey of 600 miles to the school that he might get a Christian wife, but God saw fit soon to deprive him of his new treasure. She was taken ill and died. He wrote: "Her end was peaceful and happy, though she had so wished to be useful to the people at Nagpore."

Mrs. Mullens was cheered at this time by the conversion of a girl of whom she thus wrote: "On our return from a long tour we were told that our native doctor who had so long attended to the sick on our missionary premises had died. He left behind him an old widowed mother, his own widow, and his daughter Beedoo, also a widow. On inquiry I found Beedoo had been left a widow at twelve years of age, and when her father saw the sad life before her, he hired a pundit to teach her reading and other acquirements. She was a singularly interesting girl, and previously to her conversion had scrupulously attended to all the rigorous rules imposed by Hinduism, had worn no ornaments, had taken food only once in twenty-four hours, and never tasted animal food, and never knowingly destroyed life. Though entirely shut up in her own house, the sick and poor came to her for aid."

Mrs. Mullens asked her if she would like to begin teaching a few girls in her own home. She joyfully assented, and ere long had a most interesting class of girls, some of whom belonged to her own high caste. Under her beloved friend's care, she was led to give her heart to God, and ultimately became a very efficient teacher.

Another case of interest was that of a young girl whose parents were inmates of the poor asylum. While they lived they permitted her to attend both the day and Sunday schools, and in this way she was led to see the sin of heathenism, and though not a convert, her mind was prepared to receive the truth. On her parents' death, she was taken possession of by some Hindu devotees, who carried her off to their haunts. She escaped from their hands, and ran to Dr. Wilson, but was watched by her former abductors, who assaulted her, and nearly succeeded in again enslaving her. Many later attempts were made to decoy her from her Christian home. These attempts were unsuccessful, and she became a happy and useful Christian.

An interesting Parsee school was opened in Bombay. Here 300 girls were found in their bright showy dresses, and skull-caps of cloth of gold, their ears, necks, arms, and in some cases noses adorned with jewels. A lady visitor hearing them singing in Guzerati "God save the Queen," was amused at the distinctly audible way in which the name Victoria was pronounced. She writes : " The Parsees, as a body, are very loyal to the crown. I thought of Her Majesty at the time, and wished she could have seen her pretty little Eastern subjects singing about her with might and main."

The Church Missionary Society had already occupied Nasik, and afterwards established a Christian village at Sharanpoor. It was an industrial settlement. A large congregation was collected, of whom 200 became communicants. The far-famed Godavery River, whose beauties have been sketched by Sir Richard Temple, when Chief Commissioner of the Central Provinces, rises a little south-west of the city. The Church missionary, Rev. J. Farrar, and his wife, shortly after their arrival, were saddened by the pitiable state of the female part of the community. On their application to the Female Education Society, a sum of money was voted to assist Mrs. Farrar, who, under great difficulties, had just began a girls' school. In acknowledging the help thus given, she writes :

"NASIK, 10*th August*, 1837.

"As yet there does not exist here the slightest desire for female education among any classes. Neither the higher nor the lower wish for any kind of mental culture, accomplishments, or useful knowledge for their daughters. Female education is in direct opposition to the current of opinion among the natives. It is a thing everywhere spoken against, and exposes those who are the subject of it to opprobrium and persecution. Though our girls' school is attended only by the lowest order of Shoodrus—a people regarded by the Brahmins with much the same feeling as those were regarded by the Jews, of whom they said : ' This people which knoweth not the law are cursed ;' yet the proud Nasik Brahmins have not thought it beneath their dignity, on many occasions, to track these poor little Shoodru girls to their homes, and threaten their parents with expulsion from *caste* should they continue to send girls to school. To postpone our efforts till the stream of opinion should turn in favour of female education, would be, I believe, to act the part of the peasant in the fable, who sat upon the banks of a river waiting for a passage till the waters should have spent themselves. We must work against the stream. Persons devoting themselves to this service must not expect to find pupils ready for them, and stretching out their hands for instruction. They must be prepared to exert all their ingenuity, all their powers of persuasion, to induce any to receive instruction. A boarding-school was soon added to the day-school, and a motley group constituted the first pupils;—the children of a wandering beggar woman, and six liberated African slaves from out of a hundred seized by our Government on board a native vessel. These children were most uncouth and forbidding in appearance and manners, and were so suspicious that they refused to touch the food placed before them till it had been first tasted by their teacher in their presence. Some Mussulmans, Hindus, and Marathis completed the first party."

The wife of another missionary wrote a touching account of the neglected low caste women and children, many of whom might be gathered in, were some lady found to teach them, but her own time and strength were sorely overtaxed. Among the children she had taken was a tiny widow of six, who, day after day, would sit in a corner of the compound and cry, saying: "I know I am a widow and despised by all;" while a bright girl uttered this reproof: "Jesus Christ loves little children. I pray to God every day and night through Jesus to give me a new heart, and God hears me. Will the sahib baptise me?" Famine orphans were subsequently admitted into schools in different parts of the presidency, and there was scarcely one of the band to whom some tragic tale did not attach itself. Friends in England undertook the support of several who received names chosen by their benefactors, often in remembrance of some loved one "gone home."

The cost of each child was about £6 a year. What an amount of blessing that small sum represented, only those who have known the little ones in their native state can realise. It was scarcely possible to recognise in the clean tidy child, with her white skirt and combed hair, the wretched, unkempt, unclothed mass of dirt, often besmeared with red lead, which they had before seen kneeling at the gate of the temple of Hanuman, the monkey god.

Years after, when Dr. Wilson, in the zenith of his fame, was publicly spoken of as "the great Orientalist who subordinated his scholarly reputation to missionary ends, and at whose feet every missionary and student in India must sit," we find him spending his energies upon his female schools, so admirably cared for by the second Mrs. Wilson and her helpers. In a letter to the late Sir Donald M'Leod, Lieutenant-Governor of the Punjab, who himself used his influence and fortune to promote mission work, Dr. Wilson urges the importance of female education. It had been commenced amongst the Gonds in Central India by the Berlin missionaries, to whom at one time Sir Donald had given the whole of his then scanty income. Writing in 1850 of his Bombay schools, Dr. Wilson says: "A hundred and forty of our girls were collected and examined, when the bishop and Mrs. Dealtry were delighted with them, and seemed quite surprised to see the intelligent countenances of the little things, and to hear the ready way in which they replied to the questions put to them. The bishop said that he had seen nothing like it in India, and it was a scene he could never forget, and he never says what he does not feel." Mrs. Wilson had at this time upwards of 500 girls in her native schools.

The Bible women in Bombay are now exercising a great influence. They have access not only to private houses, but to hospitals and asylums, and are much blessed at the dispensary. Lately, a poor woman who had had a severe accident said: "I feel all my pains leave me when you talk. The name of your God sounds so sweetly that I feel quite satisfied. Go on. Do not stop. Do not let the noise disturb you. Let me hear." At the jail their visits to the female prisoners were at first objected to. But the women begged that they might be permitted to come and read the good words to them. One woman said: "I have spent lots of money in making vows to our gods, now I will lay my child at the feet of your Jesus. But where is He? Can you tell me?"

One word must be said as to the indirect blessings resulting from the efforts of Christian ladies in heathen lands. It is so well illustrated in Mrs. Weitbrecht's "Female Missionaries in India," that an extract may be given as a typical case. She says: "On one occasion a lady, wife of a civilian, was stopping over the Sabbath in our mission house. The delicate state of her health prevented her from attending evening church, and she remained at home with me. At the usual hour the native Christian women assembled and took their customary places on a mat on the floor. The orphan girls sat in front. The service commenced with the catechist giving out a Bengalee hymn, in which every individual joined. When the singing ceased the whole company prostrated themselves in

Oriental method, and a short fervent prayer was offered, followed by an exposition suited to the capacities of the hearers. After the concluding hymn and prayer the women and girls passed before the lady and myself in rotation, making their salaam on leaving. The lady was quite overcome, and exclaimed : 'Oh, this is true happiness! This is delightful! A missionary's wife must be indeed a happy woman!'"

Our space will not allow any record of woman's work in the Punjab, North-west Provinces, or Ceylon. In that island the Female Education Society aided the wife of Bishop Claughton, and the admirable schools of the Wesleyans, and nowhere has greater blessing been vouchsafed. Honorary workers, like Miss Tucker, Miss Reade, Miss Lowe, Miss Clay, Miss Davidson, Miss Anstey, and others, are labouring with zeal and energy, and are seeing "signs following," while the ladies associated with the various British and American societies are constantly cheered by one and another coming out of heathenism and avouching themselves followers of Jesus. In the last reports of the Woman's Foreign Missionary Society of America we have this striking testimony from the mother of a large family: "My sons tell me that the Hindu religion will not last, that even now it is tottering. How thankful I am that I and they live in the English rule, when we can learn what has been hidden from us for ages."

In Oude their Bible woman Victoria is carrying on zenana work in houses built by the old grandees of the time of the King of Oude. One family lives in the apartments of a large Mohammedan praying-place. The Americans, like their Scotch sisters, have begun in some places to take fees from their pupils, so many being now anxious to learn. What a contrast to the time when pice were obliged to be given to induce the parents to allow even children of the lowest caste to come. Truly we may say—What hath God wrought!

CHAPTER V.

INDIA—ZENANA MISSIONS.

"Captives of the mighty."—ISAIAH xlix. 25.

THE work done under this title was begun many years before the word zenana was known to most English people. Sheridan accused Warren Hastings of oppressing the "unknown begums in their secluded zenanas;" and in an interesting letter to the venerable John Newton, Dr. Claudius Buchanan says, writing from Tanjore, October, 1806: "I have seen the two little daughters of the King of Tanjore to-day. They were covered with pearls and diamonds, but cannot read one word. The king desired me to lend him a painting I had to show to his ladies, but it was three days before I could get the rajah out of his zenana." It is probable that he was the first English minister who understood the exact meaning of the name. It is a Persian word, derived from *zen*, meaning woman. In North India the inmates are called *purdahnashin*, or curtain-women—*i.e.*, sitters behind the curtain. The word means the women's apartments. The Turkish equivalent is harem or seraglio.

Zenana visitation refers to the access obtained by Christian ladies to the aristocratic and high-born Mohammedan and Hindu ladies in their own homes. Long years ago the Hindu women enjoyed comparative freedom, till seclusion was forced upon them by the perils of Mussulman rule. Since that time every woman, except those of the lower orders, has been immured in the prison walls of her home, shut off from all communication with the outer world, and in many cases never seeing the face of any man but her lord and master. A zenana mission, therefore, is simply a mission to Indian high-caste women, carried on exclusively by women.

It is often called "a new agency," and in one sense it is, for it is now carried out systematically by no less than twenty American ladies' societies, and by about half as many English.

In addition to the Female Education Society, the Church of England Zenana Society, the Indian Female Normal School Society, scarcely any missionary society is without its "Ladies' Branch," or "Women's Committee."

Besides these, Women's Missionary Societies have been established in Scotland, Switzerland, Germany, Holland, and Canada. But the work long preceded the organisation. With all this array of societies and their many workers, it is estimated, by those best able to form a judgment, that there is only one femael worker labouring amongst every million of Hindu women.

The first attempts to reach the women of India were made for the lowest classes, or, as a Government official described them, " the very dregs."

This chapter will record the commencement of Christian and educational work amongst the high-born and wealthy inmates of their prison homes.

A well-known Hindu writer, Pundit Sivanath Gastri, says : " I do not think there is a single person here who would stand up and defend this monstrous custom which has sapped the foundation of our national greatness. . . . So long as we have not been able to educate our wives and daughters, we cannot attain moral superiority. Good mothers are wanted for the regeneration of India."

To see the need for zenana work, it is well to try and realise the life of a Hindu married woman. In the first place, no man except the husband is permitted to enter a zenana. From the time of a girl's marriage, which usually takes place between eleven and fourteen years of age, when she is removed from her parent's home and taken to her husband's, she is placed by him in a zenana under the care of her mother-in-law. After that she is, as a rule, forbidden to see the face of any man. She has no education except the worship of idols. Menu states : " It is worse than blasphemy to attempt to educate a female. She was born in ignorance, she must die in ignorance." She spends her time in gossiping, dressing her hair, counting her ornaments, eating sweetmeats, and preparing food for her husband and children.

She is never allowed to eat with her husband, and always takes her meals after he has finished. Her great amusement is to teach her little ones the service of the idols[1] that are worshipped at stated times in the year. The birth of a female child is to the young mother an awful period. She does not hear the sound of the conch shell, as at the advent of a boy, and, overwhelmed with sorrow, she curses the day and curses her fate.

Polygamy is a fruitful source of misery, and a girl of five or six may often be heard indulging in all manner of curses and imprecations against her child rival.

Shib Chunder Bose, from whose book many of these facts are taken, says: "A tender girl of five is as her *first* instruction before emerging from her nursery initiated into the brata or religious vow, the primary object of which is the ruin and destruction of a rival wife." The same author mentions that in many cases opium is taken to end their misery.

No woman after marriage is allowed to utter the name of her husband. The jealousies and quarrellings in after life may easily be imagined. If such be the state of the wife, what is that of the widow? Then indeed her cup of misery is full.

An educated Hindu lady thus writes: "O Lord, why hast Thou created us to make us suffer thus? From birth to death sorrow is our portion. While our husbands live we are slaves; when they die we are still worse off. O God! I pray Thee let no more women be born in this land."

[1] See Bose's "Hindus as they Are."

Another writes: "Our Queen Empress is a widow, can she not help us? The Sahib-log did away with suttee, but it was less cruel than this long, lingering torture. Would that I could die! Any life is better than this; even an animal, a worm, is less miserable."

Another native lady writes: "We are prisoners and long-life sufferers. Hearing of our condition the eyes of strangers fill with tears. But you leave us there. Have you no pity in your hearts?"

Perhaps the most touching cry that has ever reached British women comes in the form of a "Hindu Woman's Prayer." The whole may be found in "Thy Cry at Night and Song at Sunrise," by A.L.O.E., one of the lady missionaries working at Batala, who has devoted time, talents, fortune, and life to lead some of her Eastern sisters to Jesus.

We can only find space for a short extract. It begins thus: "O Lord, hear our prayer! No one has turned an eye upon the oppression which we suffer, though with weeping and crying, and desire, we have turned to all sides hoping that some would save us. No one has lifted up his eyelids to look upon us, or to inquire into our case. Thou art the only one who will hear our complaint. O Lord! inquire into our case! . . . O Father! when shall we be set free from this jail? O Lord! for what sin have we been born to live in this prison? O Thou hearer of prayer! if we have sinned against Thee, forgive; but we are too ignorant to know what sin is. O great Lord! our name is written with drunkards, lunatics, imbeciles, and infants; with the very animals! As they are not responsible, we are not. Criminals confined in jails are happier than we are, for they know something of the world. They were not born in prison. It is, to us, nothing but a name; and not having seen the world, we cannot know Thee, its Maker. O Father of the world, dost Thou care only for men? Hast Thou no thought of us women? O Lord! save us, for we cannot bear our hard lot. Many of us have killed ourselves, and are still killing ourselves. Our prayer to Thee is—that this curse be removed from the women of India."

Mrs. Murray Mitchell states that one poor creature in a zenana, while deploring their condition, used this singular comparison: "The life we lead is just like that of a frog in a well. Everywhere there is beauty, but we cannot see it."

These women suffer more than all others from the blight of heathenism. Taken from their homes when mere children, sold in infancy to the highest bidder, and often widowed before they understand the very meaning of the word, their life is one long chapter of wretchedness.

A missionary lady noticed a pale, woe-begone looking child of thirteen, who always during her visits sat in a corner and wept. Inquiring the reason, this touching answer was given: "I am hated, scorned; no one cares for me. I was a widow at three years old! Truly such a life is a living martyrdom." Amongst the blessings of English rule has been the abolishing of suttee, but it is not a matter of surprise to find that there are still those who regard it as a questionable boon. In a number of the "Indian Female Evangelist" is a translation of a paper written by an inmate of a zenana, who has so far profited by the instruction of the white lady that she has attempted to write a book! One paper in it is headed, "Hindu Widows: by One of Themselves." Of course its facts apply to that part of the country, and the particular caste of the lady herself, into which we have no desire to pry. It is considered by some old residents in India as one of the fullest and truest accounts ever published. The writer says that her caste being high, the customs are enforced with great rigour, although when the widow is the mother of a son she retains more influence.

The moment the husband has drawn his last breath, six wives of barbers, who are kept ready, rush upon the widow and strip her of all her ornaments. Trinkets plaited into her hair are dragged out, earrings and nose-rings wrenched off, so as often even to tear the cartilage. The gold armlets are hammered with a stone till the metal breaks. And all this even if the widow be but a child of six or seven years old. At the funeral procession she is dragged along by the barbers' wives, and not allowed to approach within 200 feet of any other woman, for woe to the wife on whom should fall her shadow; she would soon be a widow too! Passers-by are warned to keep out of the way of the accursed thing. When at length the procession has reached the bank of the tank or river on which is prepared the funeral pyre, the widow is pushed into the water. It matters not what the weather, there she has to be till the body is consumed; and not only so, but till all the party have bathed, washed, and dried their clothes. Then, when all are ready, she is pulled out as she was pushed in. She walks home in her dripping clothes. Can we wonder that the zenana widow often exclaims: "Oh, I would far rather choose the suttee!"

She states that before she herself was a widow, she had to be present at the funeral of a near relative. For nine hours the poor widow was kept in the blazing sun and hot blasting wind. Had she asked for a draught of water her character would have been gone! At last she fell. They dragged her up, but finally she could no longer crawl. They pulled her along till they arrived at the house. She was flung upon the floor. The writer then says: "After the funeral every widow is put into a corner, and there has to sit or lie on the ground in perfect silence; but if *her* lips are closed, those of her friends around her are opened." Her mother says: "Unhappy creature, I wish she had never been born!" The mother-in-law says: "The viper! she has bitten my son and killed him." Her sister-in-law says: "I will not look at or speak to such a thing!" For thirteen days must the widow sit thus on the floor in the clothes in which widowhood overtook her, those damp clothes in which she lay while her husband's body was being burned. Only once in twenty-four hours is she allowed to touch food, and then only bread and water. She may not speak, she may not even weep. No marvel that many die as the result of this treatment.

On the eleventh day, the Brahmin priest comes to demand from her money, oil, and other things, as death dues. Often do widows have to labour for months at grinding corn to pay these dues.

Thirteen days after the death the relations assemble. The widow cannot inherit from husband or father. So each relation brings something, to which are added reproaches. This money is to be her portion for life. Her hair is then all shaven off. The robes she wore when the doom fell upon her are taken off, and the unchangeable widow's robe put on. In addition to the privation of any second meal, she has to observe certain fasts, during which the poor creature often tastes nothing for forty-eight hours. This zenana widow adds: "I once saw a widow die. She was one of my cousins. When her husband died, she was lying ill of a burning fever. Immediately she was thrown from the bed on to the floor. Lying there till the moment came for the funeral to start, she was incapable of moving to take her place. The mother-in-law called a water-carrier, and had four skins of water poured over her as she lay upon the ground. At the end of eight hours death brought the family the welcome opportunity of praising her, which they did, saying 'she had died for love of her husband!'" "The English," this writer adds, "have abolished suttee. Alas! neither the English nor the angels know what goes on in our homes. Thousands of us die, but more live. Nearly every man or boy who dies leaves one, often more. I am told that in England they comfort the widows, but there is no comfort for us." This touching story, written by one of India's daughters, recalls the burning words of the late Bishop Vidal, in a sermon preached on behalf of the Female Education Society, in Portman Chapel, in the year 1852. "Think," he said, "of the unequalled sorrows of the Eastern female. Do we not everywhere behold her a mourner, an outcast, degraded, trodden down, insulted, uncared for? A prisoner and a slave. Jealously guarded by her domineering lord, and tutored to become his senseless plaything; or the abject servant of the poor man, in silent submissive servitude, performing every menial office and drudgery for him without one syllable of thanks; never sitting in his presence, or venturing to partake of any meal with him; dragging on for years a life of misery so insupportable, that death itself were infinitely preferable. A life of helpless, hopeless anguish, looked on by all around her as a cursed thing, a grovelling wretched creature, fit only to be spurned and trodden under the foot of man. Such is the career of hapless woman wherever Brahminism exerts its sway in India."[1]

One of the lady speakers at a meeting convened to give information on the subject, truly said: "We have, as a nation, taken our religion and education to the men; and the wives and mothers are brokenhearted. They are weeping, while the men, especially the young men, are laughing at the old gods, and turning them into derision. In thousands of cases it is

---

[1] It is well always in reading missionary accounts to bear in mind the vastness of the field, and the difference of national habits in different parts. If customs practised in the North of England are unknown in the South, how much greater must be the variation in such an extensive country as India. And yet every fact stated may be perfectly true. This applies to zenanas as well as to other places and things.

their tears and entreaties that have caused husbands and sons to be false to their convictions."

A Church without women is, as it has been truly said, an impossibility. Whilst all false religions thrust women out of their systems, Christ's religion raises and ennobles them, and makes them nursing mothers to His Church. One convert said to a missionary lady: " Do you know why we have so opposed Christianity? Just because we did not know it. Now we find it is a religion of love, we can no longer warn them against it."

Another having heard some chapters in the Gospels, said with earnestness: " Do you know I think your Jesus must have been a woman. He speaks so lovingly."

It affords one of the many instances in which He who is Lord of all causes the wrath of man to praise Him, that ever since the mutiny, the ladies connected with all the different missionary societies have found more ready access to the high caste women of India. When Mrs. Mullens, who has been called "the Apostle of the Zenana Mission in Bengal," began her work in Calcutta in 1857, she and Mrs. Sale stood alone in the face of many difficulties. Now, with multiplied labours the open doors greatly outnumber those who are found to enter them.

In the present day it is difficult to realise the difficulties encountered by the pioneers in zenana work. It was begun quietly, almost secretly, and was opposed by the women themselves almost as much as by the men. The workers required the wisdom of the serpent united with the harmlessness of the dove. They went conscious of their own weakness, but confident of success, because trusting in Almighty power.

These female messengers of the King had heard much of the sorrows hidden behind those *purdah* walls, but the description did not equal the reality. Nothing but the direct command of the Master, and His own "sure word of promise" could have sustained them in their early difficulties and disappointments. It was only by the direct permission of the head babu, and the burra bow, or head zenana lady, that an entrance could ever be obtained, and when once admitted to the apartment, the inmates hurried to the furthest end, gathering their *chuddars* closely round them to prevent possibility of the garment coming in contact with the Christian visitor.

The skill of some of these ladies in needlework was one of the means by which access was first gained to their Indian sisters. A native gentleman, visiting a missionary, was struck with the pretty slippers, hand screens, and other articles which met his eye, and more so still when told they were made by the white man's wife and sister. "I should like my wife taught such things," was the reply. The suggestion was thankfully caught at, and thus access to a zenana was obtained. Mrs. Mault, of Nagercoil, gained a footing in several by instructing the ladies in the art of lace-making.

It is a curious fact that after so many years this industry still flourishes in that locality.

One of the early agents of the Female Education Society accompanied the late Rev. A. F. Lacroix and his wife to Chinsurah, simply as a school teacher, where more than 100 children were gathered under her care. But as she was amongst the first to undertake zenana visitation, although it was not then called by that name, she shall tell her own tale.

Miss Margot writes: "Some weeks ago a rich native, a babu, came and asked me to instruct his wife. It was arranged that I should go the next day. On reaching the dwelling where these miserable women pass their useless life, I felt a grief and compassion which I cannot express. I was accompanied by one of my girls. After having passed through two or three dark passages, we came to the women's apartments, entered by no foot of man except the master of the house. After waiting some minutes the lady made her appearance accompanied by women who, I suppose, were her servants. She was literally covered with jewels, having at least thirty bracelets of massive gold, and I know not how many chains of gold and precious stones round her neck, to say nothing of a large ring enriched with an immense pearl attached to the right nostril. After having fully examined me, she began to put many childish questions, among others why I did not wear jewels. At length, in my turn, I asked her if she would like to learn to read. 'What good would it be?' she replied. 'Why should I take so much trouble?' 'Well then,' I said, 'would you not like to learn to work?' Again she answered, 'And what good would it be to learn to work? I can buy all I want.'

"Her husband, who was listening behind the door, said, 'You see my wife is stupid, she will learn nothing; but when my little girl is old enough I will give her to you, and you will do with her as you like.'"

Very quietly and unostentatiously these ladies—amongst whom Mrs. Lacroix and her daughter, Mrs. Mullens, held a conspicuous place—worked in these hitherto unknown abodes. The wonderful talents and doings of the white ladies were whispered from one to another, and slowly but surely access was gained to them. Some amongst the happiest of these lady prisoners were content with their lot; satisfied with dressing the hair, counting jewels, or playing with dolls; but others pined for something better. To such the visits of the missionary lady were a source of unmixed delight. They forgot their miserable surroundings in listening to the wonders told by their new friends, and in examining the pictures, fancy work, and other marvels brought by them. In many zenanas grown-up ladies were found playing with dolls like children. These they often dress up and adorn with real jewellery. In a zenana visited by a missionary lady, the family had spent the equivalent of £25 in English money to celebrate the coming of age of a doll!

Dr. Duff, than whom no one was better acquainted with the state of feeling in India, wrote from Calcutta: "You know the *almost incredible difficulties* connected with female education in this part of India. The intense desirableness no one with a Christian heart can doubt. The zenana or *home* domestic scheme, which at first failed, and is again attempted by Mrs. Fordyce, ought to present the most inobjectionable form of instruction to the native mind. The great difficulty in *day schools* is getting the girls conveyed to and from school." Referring to the first of his own girls' schools, which began with two and increased to twenty, Dr. Duff goes on to say, "that after a few weeks it is threatened with total extinction." A rich Kulin Brahmin, hearing that his poorer cousin had let me some rooms for the school, assembled a crowd at the house, and poured upon him a torrent of invectives for bringing disgrace upon the whole family by sanctioning so shocking an innovation, and launched out with vehement threatenings, if he did not instantly shut the door against me and the poor little girls. That he had the power greatly to harass and perhaps utterly ruin him was undoubted. He then threatened the parents, so that not half-a-dozen girls were left. But I continued to reply: "So long as one single girl remains, she shall be taught." At length we had between forty and fifty in daily attendance.

It is cheering to note the gradual improvement in the inmates of these Hindu homes. The writer remembers one of the pioneers in this good work, years ago, telling her that it was some time before the native ladies would allow her to touch, or even come near to them. In each case a line was marked out, and the visitor approaching it laid down the baby's dress, or slippers, she wished to exhibit, and then retreated to the further end of the apartments. Some slaves would take the articles up, and bring them to the divan for their mistress to examine, and this done, would return them to the same place on the floor, when the missionary lady would take them up, and place others in their stead. By degrees the visitor was allowed to come nearer, and then followed the interesting examination of every article of her dress,

F

always accompanied by the same question: "Are you married?"

A Barrackpore lady says: "Now it is no longer the women are hard to get at, but just the simple want of some one to go to them. The strong prejudices are giving way. Even the babus invite us in."

Infanticide is a frequent and common result of the degradation felt by the Hindu women. They bewail the birth of a daughter as a great calamity. Harrowing tales can be told by the zenana visitors in proof of this.

One young mother only expressed the views of thousands when she significantly told her English visitor: "Surely it was a great kindness to *allow* the baby girl to die." Our Government has forbidden open infanticide, and the infants are not now as of old cast into the river to propitiate the Goddess Gunga, but child murder still has its secret victims in many a native home. The cruel custom of casting the mother, ere her baby sees the light, into some dark dirty shed in the courtyard, or, as our friends can testify, into a damp cow-house, makes such murders very easy of accomplishment.

So wretched is the Hindu lady's lot that suicide is no unfrequent occurrence. In an account given by Mrs. Greaves, a lady missionary, we read that as she was passing a zenana one day she heard that the babu was in mourning for his wife. Asking the cause of her death, the answer given was, "she had had a quarrel with her husband, had sent out for opium and poisoned herself." Mrs. Greaves added: "I asked if this was a rare event, and was answered,

'Oh no! if a woman is unhappy she knows she must die sometime, so she just poisons herself to get out of her trouble quickly.'"

One of the first publications that directed attention to the subject in England was a little book written in 1826, called "A Voice from India," containing a translation from a pamphlet entitled "The Victim of Delusion; or, a Hindu Widow." But it was soon out of print, and it, and the Hindu widows, were alike forgotten.

One incident that occurred to an early zenana worker, between forty and fifty years ago, when publicity would have proved a death-blow to the work, may now safely be recorded. Through a kindly feeling conceived for her by some very young children, our friend was invited to pay a visit to one of the elder ladies of the family. Caste feeling was then so strong that though delighted to see a white woman, and full of wonder that she had no husband, not one would venture to take a book or piece of work from her hand, and, as she subsequently learned, her native friends, on her departure, sent all their outer garments to be washed, as a further protection from any defilement they might have sustained by contact with a Christian. This, she afterwards discovered, was a regular practice, not only in that family, but in others to which she subsequently gained access. When, long afterwards, she pointed to a rich silk saree worn by one of the ladies, she remarked: " Surely *that* could not be washed." "Silk is holy, and cannot be defiled," was the immediate reply. Owing to the great heat and closeness of the rooms, the ladies would sometimes offer sherbet, or some light refreshment to their guest, but the offer was always accompanied by the request that she would accept the vessel that had contained it.

Being polluted, the remainder of its contents must be at once thrown away, and the vessel destroyed. Among her pupils in one zenana was a bright young creature, wife of one of the younger sons of the house, who seemed to take a special interest whenever the way of salvation was spoken of, but not a word was ever said by her on the subject. One day the missionary teacher found the young wife in her apartment alone—a most unusual event, one that had never before happened. As soon as she had taken her place, her pupil arose from the floor, and, regardless of all supposed defilements, threw her arms round her friend's neck, exclaiming: "Oh, I am so glad you have come to-day, now I am alone. I have so wanted to tell you how I love you, because you have taught me about Jesus. I do love Him, for He has forgiven my sins, and washed them away in His own blood. He is *my* Saviour. Do come to-morrow and tell me more about Him. I shall be alone again to-morrow." At that moment a step was heard approaching, and the young wife hastily resumed her veil. It proved to be her own husband, and as he entered the room, the expression on his face, and a cold, cruel glitter in his eye, convinced the teacher that her pupil's words had been overheard, and her heart sank to think of the probable consequences. The gentleman, with hollow politeness, echoed his wife's words. "Yes, pray come to-morrow: she will be alone, and delighted to see you." He attended the lady to the door, and repeated the invitation. She went the next day, and found her worst fears were realised. The husband met her at the entrance, and with an icy smile and ill-concealed triumph said: "You will not see her again; she sleeps." Yes, she did sleep: but it was the sleep that knows no waking. It was subsequently known that she had been poisoned, or murdered in some other way. The youthful martyr had sealed her testimony with her life. Teacher and pupil have long ago gone to their rest. Good and faithful servants, they have "entered into the joy of their Lord."

Well may a native of high caste write: "See in what a life of drudgery and misery our mothers, wives, and daughters live." It is not we Christians alone who have painted the black picture; it is the verdict of their own nation. In the Hare Prize Poem, written by a Bengali lady, we have these touching lines:—

> "On like purchased slaves we go;
> Ah! dost Thou then mean it so?
> Still, although the heart is broken,
> Must the pang remain unspoken?
> Veil the face and hide the woe,
> Ah! dost Thou then mean it so?
> Wretched custom's helpless slaves,
> 'Whelmed in superstitious waves.
> Thus our precious life doth go:
> Ah! dost Thou then mean it so?"

CHAPTER VI.

BATAVIA AND BORNEO.

"The beloved Persis, which laboured much in the Lord."
ROMANS xvi. 12.

THIS little work would be incomplete did it not give a short sketch of the life and labours of the first lady missionary of the Society for Promoting Female Education in the East. When the newly formed committee were seeking direction both as to the choice of workers and their sphere of labour, an earnest appeal came from Malacca, from the Rev. W. H. Medhurst, of the London Missionary Society. Miss Wallace, who sailed in 1823, had already opened five schools there. Mrs. Dyer had also opened two at Penang. Mr. Medhurst wrote as follows: "I trust the work of your new society will be crowned with the happiest results. Providentially an agent is set at liberty well acquainted with the Chinese and Malay languages, both spoken

and written. Mrs. Whittle (a widow) has already written a work in Chinese. You will, I hope, secure her valuable assistance at Singapore, Malacca, or Batavia. In answer to your queries about the station, I may say that Batavia contains a population of 20,000 Chinese and 180,000 Malays. We have schools for boys, but none for girls. I have no doubt that female schools may be set up. The Dutch Government never interferes with our labours among the Chinese nor the Malays, as long as we are prudent. No assistance, however, is to be looked for from the Dutch Government."

An additional helper being required, the committee were directed to Miss Eliza Thornton. She had laboured diligently in the island of Corfu, under the superintendence of the late Rev. R. Leeves, and was from circumstances free to enter upon a fresh engagement. She seemed by her previous training and special qualifications—being well acquainted with the infants' and British school systems—to be just the agent needed.

After a solemn valedictory service she took leave of her English friends, and on 11th August, 1835, landed in Batavia Roads. Finding that two months must elapse ere she could proceed to Malacca, she at once began to help Mrs. Medhurst, who had established a boarding-school for boys and girls, and also an orphan asylum in Batavia, in which the children were taught English. Their parents were Dutch or Malay. Prayer and labour soon enabled her to speak in Malay; but the desire of her heart was to reach the Chinese. When the ports subsequently were opened, several of the missionaries, including those stationed at Malacca, left the Straits, and so Miss Thornton continued her happy work at Batavia. Help was also sent by the new society to workers in Siam, Macao, Java, and other young missions, some of which have been since left for more promising fields.

After a few months she wrote: "I have commenced school with twenty girls, and can already ask for most things that I want in Malay; but China is the object of my ambition, and I shall lose no time in attempting Chinese. My schoolroom is a bamboo roof without walls, close to a coffee plantation, and surrounded with cocoa-nut trees and plantains. Supplied with an occupation which has interest sufficient to fill the heart to overflowing, you can suppose me to be one of the happiest of human beings. I visited the boys' Chinese school, when the master—a fine old man, with a white beard—laughed, and seemed highly delighted to see an English lady. When repeating their lesson the children turn their backs upon me, as it is not considered respectful to look a teacher in the face. When anyone asks after my welfare, say I would not return for the sake of every earthly blessing.

"My work is my pleasure, my delight; of what use is life but to promote our Redeemer's glory?"

Later on, she tells of the formation of three Chinese schools, containing thirty girls, and adds: "My most promising child has just been taken away. I went to inquire the reason. The mother said because she was too old, and must now be shut up. The infant school system is here especially necessary, as no girl, after eleven years of age, is permitted to be seen out of her house without her mother's special permission until she is married."

Soon after, Miss Thornton adopted the two orphan children of a Frenchman who married a Malay. Both were people of very bad character, and the girls were rescued from a life of sin and misery and trained to be native teachers. "Emma," she says, "accompanies me to the school at Cornelius, and is beginning to be interested in the improvement of the little Chinese girls."

At the commencement of 1837 the American and London Societies had established five other schools. More labourers were wanted, and Miss Hulk, a young lady from Amsterdam, after a training in England, was engaged to help Miss Thornton.

A committee of ladies anxious to aid this good work had been formed in Geneva, and they sent funds towards the Dutch missionary's support. Meantime Mdlle. Combe, a Swiss girl, was so impressed with the accounts of the work which reached her in her quiet home at Strasburg, that she wrote offering her services to the committee. Her simple, ardent piety, the vivacity of her spirits and manner, and great intelligence, won the hearts of her new English friends, and as a lady was now required for the native schools in Batavia, she was selected for the post, and sailed in the summer of 1838. In her voyage out she wrote: "Contentment brightened the present; hope, the future." On landing at the port of Angier, they were hospitably received by the president, and, after a few days' rest, started in a native carriage, drawn by four wilful untrained ponies, for Batavia. "Sometimes," she says, "we had to stop, because they could not drag the carriage over the muddy places; and we had to cross three miles in boats. The poor, dirty, half-naked Malays, with their basket-like hats and black teeth, look so weak and effeminate with their long hair. At first sight they all look like women. On our stopping at Mrs. Medhurst's door, the first sounds I heard were the voices of some Chinese girls learning to read. I asked if they would shake hands with me; they looked very shy, but one having collected all her courage, stepped forward, and when she returned alive and unhurt, the rest came to do the same. I approached Miss Thornton with a beating heart. Her example had inflamed me with a holy emulation. I expected much, and found more. Her life is a life of self-denial, and yet her 'face is washed, and her head anointed;' she forbears as forbearing not. In Miss Hulk, too, I find a devoted and affectionate companion. Now I am learning the language with all my might. In the afternoon I help in Mrs. Medhurst's school, and though I can only speak in broken sentences, with my Lord's help, I get on pretty well. On Sunday I have a class in the English Sunday school, and long to have one also for the Malays. I cherish the hope that by-and-by I shall have a Chinese school. But to be faithful *to-day* is my most pressing business."

These efforts made for the Chinese women in the Straits bore fruit in after years. Several, who had first learnt the truth in the Chinese villages near Batavia, carried the news of "the doctrine" back to China proper, when political changes induced many families to return to the land of their birth.

One rich Chinaman, living at Cornelius, was so struck with the change in the girls attending the school, that he promised to send his own little one as soon as ever she was old enough.

"Do exert all your influence," wrote Miss Thornton, "to interest praying Christians at home in these schools. I do not fear but that I shall be able to support them, if my friends at home are punctual in sending out articles for sale, as my adopted children are fast growing into women, and cost me a good deal for clothes. I have fourteen boarding and eleven day pupils, and am obliged to refuse many applications."

When Miss Hulk sailed to join Miss Thornton, she was accompanied by two other ladies. One was Miss Aldersey, who first began work at Sourabaya, a Dutch settlement in Java, and subsequently at Ningpo, of whom more will be heard in the chapter on China. The third of the little party was Miss Theodosia Barker, who was commissioned to assist Mrs. Gutzlaff at Macao. She subsequently became the wife of the Rev. W. Dean, at Bangkok, in Siam. This young missionary heroine died on her twenty-fourth birthday, from an attack of small-pox. Her last labours were for the heathen. On the morning of her attack, she took her class, and then read at the Chinese family worship. Prompt remedies were used, but in a few days she succumbed. The last one she was privileged to lead to the feet of the Saviour was her little Fanny's Chinese nurse. Mr. Dean wrote: "She had laboured and prayed for nurse daily, and now she prays like a Christian."

We must now return to Mdlle. Combe. After

labouring amongst the women of Borneo with Miss Thornton, she married the Rev. W. Thomson, of the American Missionary Society, and removed with him to the island of Borneo, to labour amongst the Dyaks. It is an interesting fact, that at a meeting of the Society for the Propagation of the Gospel, held on the 2nd May, 1846, the Archbishop of Canterbury stated, that he believed that "Borneo offered the most promising opening for extending the knowledge of Christ among the heathen that was to be found on the face of the earth." In a letter from the Bishop of Calcutta, after spending some time at Sarawak, dated January, 1851, he confirmed this statement, and said: "It is my full persuasion that there is no mission on the face of the earth to be compared with that of Borneo. It has been thrown open to Christian enterprise almost by miracle. As I looked at the neat wooden edifice (the church) and its Christian congregation, of whom eleven were Dyak and Chinese children, my heart was almost too full to proceed. Nothing of a secular and merely external success is to be aimed at. The salvation of souls by the atoning sacrifice of Christ, and the sanctifying grace of the Holy Spirit, must be the object in view. Christ our Lord must be preached and honoured in all the simplicity of the Gospel, or no spiritual good will follow. It is a great thing to have mission house and schools. Persevering efforts must be made to make the case thoroughly known through the length and breadth of Protestant England." May this appeal from one who "being dead yet speaketh," result in a fresh effort to bring the heathen women of Borneo to a knowledge of the Saviour, and raise up fresh lady workers!

It may be well here to state that, from the formation of the Society for Promoting Female Education in the East, the committee required each lady engaging in missionary work to sign an agreement, attested by two witnesses, and having the binding force of a legal instrument, guaranteeing the Society against pecuniary loss in the event of marriage, before the completion of their five years' term of service. They felt it would be a want of faithfulness to the trust reposed in them if, receiving funds for a specific object, they allowed them to be diverted to others, however good and desirable. This rule, though objected to by some, has been found after forty-eight years' trial to work well. Many missionary ladies have stated that they highly value it, as vindicating them from suspicion of interested motives. The length of service of several of the labourers, in some cases between twenty and thirty years, and the names of those who have died at their posts, abundantly prove that the work was undertaken from love to Christ, and love to the souls He died to save.

It has been urged that the rule should be relaxed when the ladies marry missionaries. The answer is that it is the design of the Society to maintain a *distinct agency* for a specific purpose. It must also be borne in mind that the committee is pledged to bring the agents home in case of failure of health, under medical advice, and to meet such contingencies a special fund of not less than £750 has been allotted.

Mrs. Thomson was not idle in her fresh sphere, and soon had collected so many children that she applied to friends in England and Geneva for a helper. Miss Poppy was sent, and her long years of hallowed toil prove that she was a chosen vessel sent by the Lord. They found the Dyaks sunk in degradation, "as many as twenty families living huddled together in one miserable dwelling; the elders wearing scarcely any clothing, the children none at all."

The death of Mrs. Thomson and other missionaries' wives, and many changes in the missionary circle, obliged Miss Poppy to leave the island; but she lived many years to labour for the souls of heathen women, in whose cause she spent all the best years of her life.

Some scattered references to different missions in these islands may be found in Wallace's interesting book entitled "The Malay Archipelago."

From the volume called "Statistics of Protestant Mission Societies," we quote the following observations: "It is much to be regretted that we possess so little information about the Dutch and German missions in Sumatra, Java, Borneo, and the islands of the Archipelago generally. The fact is, we know nothing comparatively of this most interesting part of the world." Wallace says: "To the ordinary Englishman it is perhaps the least known part of the globe. Scarcely any travellers explore it. In many collections of maps it is almost ignored. Few persons realise that, as a whole, it is comparable with the primary divisions of the globe, and that some of its islands are larger than France or the Austrian empire."

CHAPTER VII.

SINGAPORE.

"Witnesses unto Me."—Acts i. 8.

THIS important station demands special notice. In Egypt and elsewhere the seed has been sown with as yet but little fruit. Singapore presents one of the most encouraging instances of the success with which God has crowned the labours of His praying handmaidens. More than forty years ago it was laid upon the hearts of some ladies in Huddersfield to undertake some definite work in behalf of their heathen sisters. For this purpose they guaranteed to the Society for Female Education in the East the sum of £100 a year for at least ten years. Singapore was the station selected. Mrs. Dyer, the devoted wife of a missionary, had established a boarding school of twenty Chinese girls. But her health and other duties led her to desire that a lady should come out who could devote her whole time to the work. Several volunteered, but obstacles arose, till in 1840 two sisters apparently well qualified sailed for that distant port. The health of the younger so completely broke down that her sister found no alternative but to bring her home. Thus the prospect again darkened. But the brave-hearted Yorkshire ladies, though cast down, held to their purpose, resolving to await in patience the guidance of God's providence. The choice was at length made of one who, to her life's end, fully justified the hopes of her most sanguine friends.

Miss Grant's views on the undertaking are shown in the following lines penned on her voyage :

"Tuesday we had a storm. The dead lights were put in, mainsail split, mainmast snapped; the vessel dashed about like a plaything. The captain feared one sea after another might overtop us. Again and again I lifted up my heart in prayer. My feelings were strange, but I was not afraid. I felt at peace with God, and committed myself to Him for life or death. My whole soul was filled with the thought that before night I might have exchanged the cross for the crown; might have seen my Saviour, and entered into everlasting rest. I never felt all the promises of God more precious, nor His presence more with me."

Miss Grant reached Singapore on the 29th July, 1843, and began school the very next day, "utterly worn out with the inactive life on board ship." She adds: "I have engaged an able teacher, and intend to speak, read, and write Malay easily before I dismiss him. I can only say 'the lines are fallen unto me in pleasant places,' and the prayers of my best friends are fully answered." From the first, the Chinese girls showed a great desire to learn, and many could soon read in the New Testament, and evinced an interest in the 'new doctrine.' Later on, Miss Grant found that one girl conducted worship with several others before retiring to rest, and some of them appeared quite overcome with a sense of their sins.

The next year she wrote : "We have one girl about fifteen, who I have no doubt has believed unto salvation. She is naturally selfish and sulky. This being the case has enabled me more clearly to discern the warfare she is waging in God's strength against her own natural corruption. Another girl, who had a painful illness, said one day, 'I don't know how to be patient any more.' On asking, 'Were one of you sure of dying to-morrow, what would you do to-day?' another girl replied, 'I would be getting my grave ready'—a very important business with the Chinese—when the first girl earnestly said, 'I would believe *strongly in Jesus.*' My school is my pleasant work and my comfort. Never did teacher and pupils love each other more. I have now twenty-six souls looking to me for probably the only instruction they will receive during their lives. Pray for me that I may be faithful. There are *seven* of whom I have a good hope. Living alone, as I am obliged to do just now, is rather a trial of courage, for the Chinamen are fond of paying midnight visits. But my faithful black Madras man sleeps outside my door with a drawn sword to protect me. I hope, too, he is a Christian. The new year was a sifting time for my dear girls, and many of them stood the test in the endurance of parental wrath and beatings in a way that has made my heart leap for joy, and shown that there was an incipient martyr's spirit in them. Chunneô and her younger sister Hanĉô have become monitors. The Neô added to their names is not part of them, but merely an equivalent to our Miss. These girls have had a small plantation a short distance from Singapore left them by their father, and Hanĉô took the idols stuck up by the labourers in various parts of the garden, and dashed them to the ground, pointing out to the astonished men the powerlessness of the idols to help or defend themselves. This act might have brought her into trouble had she not been a girl of the highest caste."

Miss Grant's next step was to commence little Bible readings in the houses of some of the mothers, with her girls as interpreters. The numbers so increased (with men listening outside), that by the advice of the chaplain, the Rev. W. Humphrey, a billiard room in the compound was transformed into one for Christian services. The school soon became a central point for helping waifs and strays. Of six infant slaves subsequently rescued on board ship and brought to Miss Cooke, one died of cholera, one from the cruel treatment she had received, and the other four are all now working usefully as the wives of catechists of the Church Missionary Society. From the first the Chinese girls' school has been entirely free, for the parents are too poor to pay.

A year later Miss Grant writes: "I have still to thank God. Those that did run well are evidently going from strength to strength. English is as yet a great effort to them fully to follow; yet on a Sunday afternoon these girls bring me passages which they have voluntarily learnt. In those they choose, I see a great deal of character revealed. Chunneô, my young, happy Christian, with her merry heart, brings verses full of the joy of the Lord being her strength. Haneô repeats such Psalms as 'Hide not Thy face from me.'"

These girls corresponded with some of those under Miss Aldersey's care. The following is a translation of one of the letters:—

"MY DEAR RUTH,—Your letter made us very glad. We thank God for having helped us, and given us a teacher to teach us how we may get a blessing for our souls. Moreover, He has helped us to believe on the name of Jesus Christ. When you were in Singapore, we knew not one thing. O my friend! what you say is true. Yes, we are all sinners; nevertheless, the Lord Jesus Christ came to die instead of us. We pray to God night and morning to bless you. You must also pray for us. O my friend! pray to God for our mother. When you were in Singapore we worshipped stones. But see the kindness of God— He helps us to believe on the Lord Jesus. O pray for us and our mother, and all the girls in Miss Grant's school; for there are some who believe in the name of the Lord Jesus, and there are some who do not. . . . Give my salaams to yourself first, and your teacher, and sister, and to all whoever loves the Lord Jesus Christ.—I am your true friend, HANEÔ."

Miss Grant in another letter says: "I confess I am amazed at Haneô. She collects the children round her, and not only teaches, but exhorts them, with strong crying and tears, to receive the truth. Last Sabbath evening when I returned from service it was eight o'clock. The children were each seated at the foot of their little cots, Hancô in the middle telling them of a crucified Redeemer's love, and then putting it to them how they could hope to escape if they neglected their present opportunities.

"Another incident, though trifling in itself, occurred last Sunday. I was standing by my venetians when I saw a nice simple-hearted child named Amay come from the verandah surrounding the house. Here she stopped, looking eagerly around, as if fearful of observation, and I feared all was not right. Judge of my pleasure when I saw this little one dart over a flower-bed and plunge herself into the midst of a thick creeping plant whose leaves almost entirely hid her. There I saw her kneel down, and clasping her little hands, I heard her in prayer. The recording angel, I feel convinced, knows all, but the only words that reached me were 'ampun,' pardon, and 'amat kasihan,' very kind. She was not above five minutes in her leafy oratory when up she sprang and darted away, singing one of their hymn tunes as gaily as a lark. None but the heart of a teacher of the heathen can fully enter into the mingled feelings that arose within me. My oldest scholars now read English and write well, embroider beautifully, and are intelligent in conversation. They now require palanquins to go to church on Sunday; the rest walk like one of our Sunday schools. You know the term of agreement with my pupils is, generally speaking, for three years. The first to leave me was Chan, who went to be married. She wept much at quitting the house, and at the prospect of her approaching wedding, which, if conducted in Chinese style, must be an idolatrous ceremony.

"I laid before her her duty, and prayed for her; more was not in my power. After a few days I went to see Chunneô, who was at that time confined to bed by sickness. She was in tears. I asked what was the matter. She replied: 'The devil has won; Chan has bowed before the idols.' Oh! these words fell heavy on my heart. My labour has been in vain. All I can tell you since is, one of my girls going in to see her unexpectedly, Chan was alone, and a Bible near her on the table. May the Good Shepherd yet recall this wanderer! Soon after it was time for my much-loved children Chunneô, Hancô, and Kaychae to leave me, with their mother, who has acted as a sort of matron. The two former have been most anxious to make an open profession of Christianity, which for the last year and a half, I have not a doubt, they have fully embraced in their hearts. Their father has been long dead, so the mother's consent was the only thing wanting in order to their being baptised. This they pleaded and pleaded for—but in vain. At last the mother became so violent whenever they alluded to the subject, that they were convinced it was in vain to ask her again. But what was to be done? The time was drawing near for their leaving, and if once they left my house unbaptised, they never would have the opportunity afterwards. I therefore laid before them, in writing, all the most painful consequences that might follow their pursuing a determined course in regard to their baptism, and bid them take time for thought and prayer, and then give me their resolution, by which I should act. I never saw a more calm, composed counting of the cost, and on Friday night, 1st August, at ten o'clock, the die was cast, and my children authorised me to request our chaplain, Mr. Moule, to baptise them publicly on the following Sunday.

"The baptisms here always take place during the evening service; and I do assure you the time from that Friday night until Sunday evening was a time of dreadful nervous tremor on my part, as well as on that of my girls. Up to that night the mother had no idea what was about to take place, for I thought it imprudent to mention it to her until the very moment was come, lest she should carry the girls off and lock them up out of my reach. I can truly say, that Sunday I spent on my knees. Nobody could help me but God, and towards afternoon I felt that I had taken hold on His strength, and His strength was made perfect in weakness.

"As the bell began for evening church, I heard my children shut themselves into their room for prayer, along with their brother, who seems deeply influenced by the example and prayers of his sisters, and who had determined to come forward with them as a candidate for baptism. We had resolved to have the carriages ready, and then I was boldly to ask the mother's consent once more. I asked her if she knew her children were going to church with me? 'Yes,' she replied, 'wherever Missie pleases to take them.' Then I was obliged to put myself in the position of a suppliant, and to tell her, while the three dear children stood behind her, the very images of terror, that we had come to the determination that they should be baptised that night; but that the one sorrow was that they must act in opposition to her authority, because she was opposing the Almighty. Her agitation was extreme while I was speaking to her; but God, I do think, gave me in that same hour what to say. In short, I did not leave her till she had given a species of consent by telling me, if *I* wished it, she could not oppose me. I thanked her warmly, bid the children do the same, and jumped into the palanquin. But I saw her come out and look at us, on which I paused, and said: 'Nomis, why should not you come too, and witness what is done?' She replied: 'If Missie likes to allow me;' and the next moment the mother and her daughters were seated beside me on our way to St. Andrew's Church. I think I never felt a more pure, holy joy in my life than as I heard the foreign-accented responses of my dear girls, as in their broken English they replied: 'All dis I steadfastly believe.' Before the girls left me I gained permission from their mother to go and fetch them every Sunday morning, to remain with me all day. The Sabbath morning after, I started at gunfire (five o'clock), and with an exulting heart brought them back. They had been up since four o'clock waiting for me. My late pupil, Chan, wrote to me saying she had committed a great sin, when at her marriage she bowed her knee to the idol, with aversion and horror. Thank God, she did not bow her heart; and she added, now her only comfort is in reading her Bible."

For a long time Miss Grant could hear nothing of Beenio—another of her Christian girls—but one day a woman told her that Beenio's mother was dead, and that her father had sold her to a man for forty dollars. The woman added no one knew what ailed the girl, for when her mother was buried she would not burn paper for her, or worship her spirit, or follow any of their customs. Some months after, in one of her visits to some people in the country, Miss Grant descried a pair of brilliant eyes peeping through a hedge, which she at once recognised. She stopped the palanquin, and out rushed Beenio. Now that her abode was discovered, Miss Grant took an early opportunity of going to her. She brought with her a large-print Testament, which was most joyfully received, and on asking whether she remembered how to read it, Beenio exclaimed: "Yes, how could I forget?" "On this," writes Miss Grant, "I opened at the tenth chapter of St. John, and pointed to the fourteenth verse, 'I am the Good Shepherd.' She read it readily, when I said: 'Yes, Beenio has *read* this, but she does not understand;' on which she looked up archly, replying: 'Yes, I know,' and immediately translated it into Malay. Still uncertain, I said: 'Well, I am glad to find you know the meaning of the words, but can you tell me who the Good Shepherd is?' 'I know that's Jesus Christ,' was her ready response, without a moment's hesitation. As I came out of the house, a mother hen had just gathered her brood together, on which I said to her: 'When you see your hen collect her chickens, what do you think of?' 'I know; I remember what I learned at school,' she replied in her broken tongue, '" As a hen gaderet her chickens under her wings, so would I have gaderd dou, but dou wouldst not."' On meeting her husband, she begged me to ask him to allow her to spend the next Sunday with me, and the meeting with Chunneô, Haneô (to say nothing of myself) was not a little joyous. I thought of Dr. Krummacher's pretty chapter on the 'Hidden Church' as I looked at Beenîo's poor little hut in the midst of the sugar plantation where it stands, and felt convinced that God was secreting one of His jewels under that thatched roof, over which I do believe He will watch as over the apple of His eye."

Miss Cooke, who succeeded Miss Grant in 1853, and Miss Ryan, her assistant, watched over poor Beenîo as far as the distance permitted. Though wanting the decision of some of the others, she loved Jesus, and in her last illness her favourite hymn was, 'How sweet the name of Jesus sounds.' On one of the mission family going to her hut with some little necessary comforts, she was found dead in her bed.

Kaychae, sister to Chunneô and Haneô, was one of Miss Grant's first pupils—a very clever girl, proud of her appearance, her family, her intellect, and her nation. She possessed much more energy than most of the others, but when her two sisters and brothers were baptised, she declared she would never disgrace her name and family by turning "Englishwoman." After her mother's death, as, contrary to national usage, she would not marry, she begged to return to Miss Grant. When, after ten years of labour, her beloved teacher was obliged to return to her native land, her one sorrow was to leave this girl still a heathen. Just before her departure, a note was laid upon her table, in which Kaychae told her that she must relieve her long pent-up feelings, and tell of the dreadful struggle which for years had been going on in her heart. She had long, she said, been fully convinced of the truth of Christianity, and could only now wonder at the forbearance of God in not cutting her off in her rebellion and sin. She concluded with begging her friend to plead with God that He would even now not scorn her, but fulfil His own blessed promise—"Him that cometh to Me, I will in nowise cast out." After much intercourse with the chaplain and Miss Grant's successor, Miss Cooke, her baptism took place.

Since then several more have openly avouched themselves to be the Lord's. An orphan home was established, and Miss Cooke commenced holding meetings for reading the Bible in the homes of several of her married Christian girls. In 1856, Miss Cooke's school was visited by the Bishop of Calcutta, when the children were examined in Scripture, grammar, general history, and arithmetic. A correspondent of a Calcutta newspaper wrote: "The answers of the girls reflected the highest credit on their zealous, faithful, and affectionate teacher, and show how much may be done for that interesting people." The words of a round they sung are worth mentioning:—

"Oh! Lord save me; teach me to know Thee, teach me to love Thee."

Some who were trained under Miss Grant are now

acting as missionaries to their countrywomen. One aged convert, quite blind, who had been baptised, hearing the Bishop was in Singapore, was led forward to where he was sitting, wishing him to pray for her. In reply to some questions it was found that she knew little more than these two great truths—viz., that she was a sinner, and that Jesus loved her. She was full of joy and peace.

Writing of this, Miss Cooke says: "The Bishop has indeed left us much to remember. He was unceasingly trying to cheer and help us. The sermon for the benefit of my mission came in our hour of need. I have now thirty-three children, and did the funds allow, believe I should have fifty." The Bishop of Victoria also visited the school, and she was cheered by the arrival of boxes of work. Did friends at home know how these tokens of Christian remembrance cheer the hearts of our lady-workers, we are confident their number would be increased. As this school is, in common with others, still needing such help, it may be well to state that the value of work sent abroad for sale by the Female Education Society in 1881, was estimated at £4134, 10s.

Another way in which valuable aid is given, is by undertaking the support of native scholars and Bible-women. The Dublin friends of the Female Education Society paid the salary of a native missionary. One who knew her well, wrote: "They could hardly find a more interesting object for their charity than this earnest, sweet, young Chinese widow, with her three little children. She is labouring hard to spread the truth among her country people. She says she prays for her Irish friends every day." Friends at home are often cheered with letters from these young native workers. The writing, spelling, and inditing of many would disgrace no English lady. Anleang, in an uncorrected report of her work, writes: "I am so glad to write you an English letter, and thank you myself for all your kindness to the Chinese Girls' School. I think you are the means of bringing us all unto the fold of Christ. I feel very glad to teach others about that Saviour who has brought me from heathen darkness to the light of the Gospel." Tempang writes: "I have ten in my class. When I came to the school I was only six, and I have been twelve years, and by God's Holy Spirit working in my heart have learnt to know and love Jesus, and I am very glad dear Miss Cooke has made me now one of her teachers."

God's blessing still rests richly upon Miss Cooke and her Singapore family. On her return after a visit to her English friends, she found the children, Miss Ryan, and her native helpers all well, and everything in perfect order. The weekly meeting in connection with the Young Women's Christian Association was attended by all her old married pupils who could leave their homes, when they gladly worked for the benefit of their poorer neighbours, both Jews and heathens.

Mrs. Murray Mitchell, while on a visit recently with her husband to the Indian churches, stated that the good work is still progressing. She says: "Only a day or two ago, I saw the delightful school presided over by Miss Cooke. We were delighted to make the acquaintance of Miss Ryan, who carries on the work with so much single-heartedness and success during Miss Cooke's absence. All the children looked bright and happy. Some of the girls are earnest Christians and Christian workers, and many trained in the school are filling positions of influence and usefulness as wives of pastors and catechists in different parts of China. It seems a centre of missionary influence in Singapore. We pray that the Lord may continue to give His blessing, and that it may more and more be a nursery of souls won for Christ."

Miss Cooke's letter, March, 1882, tells of forty-two boarders in the school, the last being a half-starved baby, found by a policeman in an open drain, and laid there to be washed into the canal when the tide rose. "Many children," she adds, "are refused admission through want of room and want of funds. We have four others entirely destitute, and shall be most thankful to any friends at home who will undertake to support them."

CHAPTER VIII.

EGYPT.

"Blessed be Egypt My people."—Isaiah xix. 25.

AT a time when all eyes are turned towards Egypt, it may be interesting to take our readers back nearly half a century, and trace the first effort in modern times to bring its women to a knowledge of the Christian faith.

A few Copts and Syrians had been led by travellers to know something of the truth, and the Church Missionary Society had sent labourers to Cairo and Alexandria, but their early work was attended with much to try and depress them. It is estimated that there are in Egypt 300,000 Copts and 4,250,000 of other natives who speak Arabic, beside some thousands of Jews and Syrians.

Surely Christians have been sadly neglectful of this once highly favoured land. What might it not have been, had those to whom the word of God was entrusted flooded it with His own truth?

Yet, while many Christians were deploring the scant success of the few labourers then in Egypt, God was fitting two ladies in their Lincolnshire home to enter upon a new line of work in that country. Miss Alice Holliday, possessed of a considerable amount of learning, had long contemplated the country of Egypt with special interest. For years she had devoted her attention to some of the severer sciences, to the study of Egyptian antiquities, and to the Arabic and Coptic languages. Her earnest desire was to consecrate herself to the intellectual, moral, and spiritual elevation of the people of Egypt, through the medium of its female population. The way being made plain, and being free from family ties, she was anxious to go out under the auspices and protection of an accredited society. For this purpose she applied to the committee of the Society for the Promotion of Female Education in the East. In company with another Christian lady, Miss Rogers, who was also a personal friend, she left England in August, 1836. Miss Rogers's pecuniary resources, with occasional aid from home, were sufficient for the support of both. Furnished with valuable introductions to consuls and missionaries, the ladies landed at Malta. Here they providentially met Mr. and Mrs. Krusé, from Cairo, the agents of the Church Missionary Society. They gave the friends every encouragement. Just before leaving Egypt they had been entreated to purchase an Abyssinian woman and child, to save them from a terrible fate. The poor woman threw herself on her knees before the missionary, supplicating him to buy her, saying: "If you buy us, we shall be with Christians." This, of course, was impossible.

On arriving at Boulak, the port of Cairo, another missionary said he hailed their advent with joy, since nothing was so much needed as a lady capable of giving an education to the high class females. By the advice of the American consul, Mr. Gliddon, they went to live under the protection of the Rev. Samuel Gobat (afterwards Bishop of Jerusalem) and his wife, who had just returned from Abyssinia.

Work was at once commenced in a girls' school which had been previously established. A native mistress, who was taught in Syria, was glad of help in the mission school. Here was found a motley group of children—Italians, Spaniards, Greeks, Syrians, Copts, and Arabs, with religions almost as varied as their nations, in all numbering eighty-five. Besides these, Miss Holliday adopted four orphans. One was an Arab, another a little Abyssinian given to her by its dying mother.

Whilst thus engaged, a new and wholly unexpected sphere of labour opened before her. On the 7th of March, 1838, she was surprised by a visit from Hekekyan Effendi, one of the officers of State, who had been sent by His Highness Mehemet Ali, Pasha of Egypt. He was charged to make a formal request that Miss Holliday would at once undertake the education of all the royal females in his harem, a hundred in number. The Effendi added: "This is only to be the beginning of female education in this country. The Pasha has much larger views, but he wishes to try the experiment first on his own family. Much depends upon his eldest daughter. Only gain her favour, and you will carry every point." Miss Holliday begged to be allowed a few days for consideration. She was already engaged in an important work, which she ought not to neglect. Her missionary friends, on being consulted, felt that it was a wonderful and providential opening. She, therefore, after much prayer, and holding herself at liberty to give up should she find that it involved anything contrary to Christian principles, consented. One wish of his Highness was that his elder daughters should soon be formed into a committee to consider the best means for extending female education throughout Egypt and his other acquired dominions.

In a letter addressed at this time to Miss Holliday by the Prime Minister, he said: "In introducing an enlightened female education into Egypt, we shall be striking at the root of the evils which afflict us. In seconding my illustrious prince in his work, I have as yet been able to trace our debasement to no other cause than that of the want of an efficient moral and useful education for our women. His Highness is pleased to command that Mrs. Hekekyan shall accompany you to the harem. Thus you will not be treated as a stranger by the Ottoman ladies. I will introduce her to you on the earliest possible opportunity, that you may proceed together to Castel Ginbarra. You will do well to take a school-usher as interpreter."

The rest of the story is best told in Miss Holliday's own words:—

"Cairo, 27th March, 1838.

"This day is among the most remarkable of my life. About 10 A.M., Mrs. Krusé, Mrs. Hekekyan, and myself, mounted on donkeys, set out for the harem. On our way we called for Captain Lyons's janissary. The Vice-Consul coming up said: 'You must take mine also for the honour of the dear old island.' Thus, preceded by the two janissaries in full dress, we started, my heart in prayer to the Lord the whole time that He would make His way plain before me. With many fears we arrived at the gate of the long avenue, which is the first door of the harem. We next came to another strong gate. Here the janissaries and donkey-men were ordered to remain, while we were waited on by several eunuchs, who, taking us through a third strong gate, ushered us into a stately saloon, where several ladies were at work. We were then shown into an anteroom, and served with coffee out of splendid cups set in diamonds. Our attendants were beautiful slaves, evidently Greek, Georgian, and Circassian.

"One brought us coffee, another sherbet, a third sugar, each having numerous slaves to attend upon her below the däis. Two little girls were then brought in to us, evidently some part of the royal family, and in a quarter of an hour an old lady high in office came to conduct us to her Highness.

"We found Nazly Hanum sitting on a high divan. Mrs. Krusé and I made our European salutation, but Mrs. Hekekyan had to prostrate herself at her feet and kiss the hem of her garments. She smilingly told us to be seated. She is a little woman apparently about forty years of age. I never saw a more piercing eye in my life. She is said to be very like her father. She immediately asked which was the teacher, and asked me several questions in Turkish through an interpreter. She wished me much to come and live in the house, saying that every liberty should be allowed me. This, of course, I declined, thanking her for the honour intended. It was agreed I should teach four hours daily—from nine to one o'clock. She was smoking the whole time."

Want of space forbids us entering into the details of this work. Miss Holliday says: "Each morning she set off, praying that the Lord would give her the needed strength for her strange mode of teaching." She continued a welcome and honoured guest, and though immediate fruit did not appear, she was enabled to persevere, leaving the result with God.

She one day mentioned that she had received from England a beautiful box of fancy work, to be presented to the royal ladies. When this was told to the Pasha, he signified his intention of being present when it was opened. "Here," writes Miss Holliday, "I saw what perhaps no other European lady ever beheld, the Pasha, Mehemet Ali, standing, like one of the patriarchs of old, in the midst of his whole family —wives, sisters, and daughters. On my entrance he smiled, and with great condescension asked how I was. He paid most attention to the orrery, and model of the Thames Tunnel. On presenting the Queen's picture, Nazly Hanum immediately asked if the Queen was married; and it was with much difficulty I made her understand that she reigned in her own right alone. When I told her that she was equal in power to any king, or, as I put it, Sultan, she seemed lost in wonder.

Some time after a letter was sent by the command of his Highness the Pasha, of which the following is an extract:—" I begin by informing you that the Pasha was extremely affected at the piety and philanthropy of the English ladies composing the Society for the Promotion of Female Education in the East, and recommended the princesses to follow their example in his dominions. I send you a box of articles of Eastern female clothing and ornaments made by the Pasha's harem as a return for the samples sent by the society. The Tarka or head scarf is his Highness Ibraham Pasha's lady's own handy-work, and is intended for her Majesty the Queen. But the desire is to be merely mentioned to you. The books you sent were forwarded to me with an order from the Pasha that I should translate them into the Turkish language. I do not flatter you when I say, that they are all very much pleased with you in the harem, and they declare English ladies are the cleverest and best-behaved of all the Frank ladies they have ever seen or heard of. I cannot too strongly recommend you to be watchful and circumspect, for the sake of your ulterior success, and that of your successors. First let the fruit ripen, then pluck it."

Enclosed was a letter from the ladies of the harem themselves. It concludes with these words: "We pray God, the Most High, that you may receive eternal rewards for your benevolent labours to augment happiness among the females of the East, and we take this opportunity to inform you that your delegate, the gentlewoman Holliday, employed in your service, has pleased us with her rare knowledge, and her exemplary conduct has laid the foundations of affection. Signed by eight of the princesses, 13th day of Ramazan, 1254."

Her Majesty Queen Victoria was not only pleased to receive the needlework referred to, but graciously presented a beautiful likeness of herself to the ladies of the royal harem, through the society. The Pasha ordered that her Majesty's gifts should be received in the most honourable manner, and every possible respect shown to the Queen's likeness. Royal carriages were sent to escort it to the palace, and it was guarded by janissaries, each bearing his silver stick of office. The box containing it was covered with our national flags.

An Egyptian society, copying the very name of that in England, was perhaps the greatest wonder of all. It was established by order of the Pasha, the patrons being the royal ladies of Cairo.

Some scientific instruments, exhibited by Miss Holliday, attracted the attention of some of the Beys. One of them, Edheem Bey, seeing the progress made not only by the princesses, but the children in the school, which our friend continued zealously to superintend, desired her also to form an infant school on the English model. It began with 150 children, and the older girls' school numbered 130, while 70 more, all Jewesses, were, through the influence of Sir Moses Montefiore, gathered in another part of the city. "What a change," she writes, "has been wrought in ten years."

Miss Holliday had now become the wife of the well-known missionary of the Church Missionary

Society, Mr. Leider, and was working, if possible, with more energy than ever. When she entered Egypt there was scarcely a woman who could read, now hundreds possessed the power, and many had the best of books to read. But this incessant labour proved too much, and for a time she broke down. "My illness," she says, "humanly speaking, arose from excessive exertion in the school and harem, having, during the hot months, to go to the Casa Dehara when the heat exceeded 114° of Fahr. The sand wind, too, and the table at the harem, added not a little to it. I have tried again and again to avoid the dishes, but nothing would do with her Highness but that those most esteemed by herself should be tasted by her teacher day by day." In 1846 Mrs. Leider wrote: "I have suffered much from ill health and blindness, having quite lost my sight for several months. The Lord, nevertheless, has been most merciful to me, for our orphan girls, through my previous instructions, were able to keep the house in order, and do all that was necessary. Had it not been for these afflictions, I should have continued to attend the harem, but I was, I believe, providentially withheld. Had I persevered, under the existing state of politics, there is no doubt I should have received a dismissal, and this was an event to be carefully avoided."

Change in Egyptian politics, and her own broken health, obliged Mrs. Leider to quit Egypt, and she did not live to return. But again God in His providence had been preparing another labourer. Nearly twenty years ago Miss Mary Whately, daughter of the well-known Archbishop of Dublin, opened her first little school in Cairo. All her friends assured her that to bring Egyptian Moslems under Scriptural instruction was an impossibility. But her faith was strong, and she believed that the things which were impossible to men were possible with God. In one respect her mission was unlike Miss Holliday's. Miss M. Whately began with the lowest. The misery of the poorer classes of women touched her heart. She often saw them shivering in their single garment of blue cotton in the early morning, as they filled their pitchers or washed their clothes on the banks of the Nile, their teeth chattering while they stood almost knee deep in the chill waters. Then in the intense heat of summer, while their lazy husbands sat and smoked under the palm trees, they would have to walk to and fro, to fetch water with immense jugs upon their heads. This toil would be exchanged for field labour, and often on their return to the place called "home," they would be beaten for some fancied neglect of duty. Her own man-servant, by no means an ill-natured man, would speak of beating his wife as a matter of course! All she at first attempted was to visit the poor women of the lower orders in their huts, or as they sat at their doors in the alleys and lanes. From such homes she gathered her first scholars. By degrees she became better known, and her skill in curing some of her little pupils, who were suffering from ophthalmia, led to requests to visit older members of the families. The curses and the handfuls of dust thrown at her became less, and at last many came to regard her as their best friend.

In time she established harem visitation, and found

some of the prison inmates willing to receive the Gospel. One woman, after listening eagerly to the story of Christ's love, exclaimed, "Oh, why was I never told of this before?" The schools became such a success that the Khedive presented Miss M. Whately with ground upon which to build schools commensurate with the increasing number of scholars. To erect these Miss Whately herself contributed largely. Her "Ragged Life in Egypt" and other works are well known to the Christian public.

Miss M. Whately saw fruit to the glory of God. Before the late war drove her from Egypt and scattered her little flock, she had reason to rejoice that many had learnt the way to heaven, and some, she had every reason to believe, were safely landed there. One of her latest letters from Cairo tells this touching story: "About three years ago a young woman, with three or four others, was sitting under the palms near her village. I had not met with a good reception. Some bigots seemed determined to break up the reading. So I retired to a palm grove, followed by a few girls and women. This young woman listened in silence, and it seemed as if she began, for the first time, to think of anything spiritual, and to feel that she had a soul. Before I left she took my hand, and said, 'Those are blessed words in your Book.' Another lamb is folded from my little flock, and, we have every reason to believe, is gone to be with Jesus. She and her sister were sent to me at four and six years old, and when old enough, each was made a pupil-teacher. They were good, and, I had every cause to hope, believing girls, and read the Scriptures well. At fourteen, the eldest, Nafesa, was married by the mother, in spite of my earnest remonstrances, to a young widower with a particularly disagreeable mother, and mischief-making widowed sister, and three ugly, spoiled, fretful children. He had a good salary as 'Katib,' or native scribe, and the foolish old woman clung to the riches and sacrificed her child. Of course, he spoke fair at first, and everything was smooth; but, after a few weeks, the poor girl was wretched, and she has, from the wedding-day until now (more than a year and a-half), never been allowed outside her door, even to visit me, and all the winter has to light a lamp after *noon*, as she has to keep the lattice shutters closed, and in a street this causes actual darkness when the full sun is off the windows! She is pale and sickly, and her infant thin and weak, of course. The second sister then fell ill, greatly from fretting; she got a bad leg, and then the disease fell on the general frame in some way, and she got what the Irish call a 'waste.' The mother had put her under a stupid native doctor, who did her no good. When our doctor's baby-son was baptised, just before the outbreak of this rebellion, this poor girl, who had been a month or more ill, managed to come riding on a donkey, though looking like a ghost, so thin and weak; I said, 'Fatmeh, you are not fit to be out!' she replied, 'I would come; I wanted to see the baptism so much!' I said, 'You ought yourself to be baptised, only I do not wish to make a disturbance and anger your mother just now; but, at any rate, tell me what you think of this when you see it.' She understood English enough to follow in part, and seemed greatly interested. At my request, the English Chaplain, who had come to baptise Dr. A——'s little boy, asked her if she believed in the Lord Jesus Christ. She answered emphatically, in her pretty, broken English, 'I do; yes, I do!' He asked one or two more simple questions, and was, he told me, satisfied that the girl was a sincere believer. Only two days after this, we had to make a sudden break up, and when I returned, after more than two weeks in Alexandria, the dear girl was dead. She had grown rapidly weaker, and for three days could not speak; but the Christian teachers were with her constantly, comforting her with texts, etc. Her only grief seemed to be that her cruel husband refused to allow her beloved sister to go and see her, though but a few doors off. Truly she is better off than if she had lived, and all know that she died a believing Christian."

Miss Whately is again in Cairo, and earnestly desires the prayers of God's people in the work so near to her heart. She writes, December, 1882: "Scholars are beginning to pour in already, more Christians at first than Moslems, but they will soon follow. With the banner of love I will go forth, and try to show that the God they ignorantly worship with fanaticism is really a God of mercy, and love, and peace; and I hope we shall see light shining in darkness before long."

CHAPTER IX.

CHINA.

"These from the land of Sinim."—Isaiah xlix. 12.

CHINA was for centuries closed to all Protestant missionary efforts. It was not till 1806 that any attempt was made to bring to its inhabitants the light of the Gospel. Then the "two-leaved gates," which had for centuries closed her in from the rest of the world, began to relax their complicated fastenings, and those devoted men Dr. Morrison and Dr. Milne and their wives, with their lives in their hands, attempted to enter them, though denied a house in China proper, and obliged to seek one in the Straits. After years of patient toil they succeeded in translating the Bible into Chinese. For long their mission was regarded as visionary and quixotic. Even Christians looked upon it as premature and hopeless. Uncheered and without sympathy, they laboured on year after year. Then foreign wars, and the domestic Taeping rebellion, weakened the prestige of their Government. At the same time the emigration of many thousands to the Indian Archipelago, Malacca, and Singapore, brought the Chinese into contact with the mind of the Western world. Subsequently Dr. and Mrs. Gutzlaff and others found their way into the Celestial Empire, and travelled from port to port, distributing portions of the Scriptures and tracts in the colloquial dialects, and taught any who were willing to learn. Mrs. Gutzlaff, who, as Miss Wallace, had been sent out by some Scotch ladies, soon applied to the Female Education Society for help. Writing from Macao, 14th December, 1836, she says: "Pray, pray, pray send us teachers heart and soul in the work. We have now twenty-three children. When will Miss —— come? Make haste and send us a helper, there is so much to do. Thousands of children to be trained, and only one solitary teacher. It is probable we shall soon remove to a more convenient house, and then I could accommodate several young female friends. I will strive to be mother, sister, friend to them." Miss Barker was at once sent. By the treaty of 1842 not only was Hong-Kong ceded to Great Britain, but the five ports were thrown open, with permission to erect churches and establish schools. But, before that time, Miss Aldersey, a lady who had from its formation been on the committee of the Society for the Promotion of Female Education in the East, had entered upon that field of labour. It had long been her cherished desire to benefit the Chinese women. A friend of Dr. Morrison, she had, under his instruction, when only nineteen years of age, diligently applied herself to the study of the language. Surrounded with all the comforts that abundant means could furnish, she endeavoured in every way possible to fit herself to endure the privations of missionary life. With her father's consent, in the year 1832, she made preparations to accompany a missionary party to the Straits of Malacca, to labour among the Chinese emigrants. But, just on the point of embarking, her plans were frustrated by the sudden death of a sister leaving six children. To her ardent mind it was a severe trial, but she saw the hand of God in it, and at once bent her energies to supply to the bereaved ones, as far as in her lay, the place of a mother. Her state of mind at that time was well described in the beautiful lines of Madame Guyon,—

> "If place I seek, or place I shun,
> My soul finds happiness in none;
> But with my God to guide my way,
> 'Tis equal joy to go or stay."

For five years all thoughts of China were abandoned. Then another was found to take her place in the family, and, on the 10th of August, 1837, she left England with Dr. and Mrs. Medhurst, and another young worker, who was early called to her heavenly rest. By their advice she settled first in Java, and opened an Indo-Chinese school. Another five years passed, during which she had, through her knowledge, ministered largely to the sick. This afforded her many opportunities of giving religious instruction, which she diligently embraced. Two of their pupils, Ati and Kit, renounced heathenism, and were baptised.

After a short stay at Singapore, she proceeded to Hong-Kong, arriving there the very day peace was proclaimed and the five ports thrown open to commerce and missionary enterprise. In 1844 Miss Aldersey, in spite of great difficulties, removed to Ningpo.

Bishop Smith, in his "History of China," thus refers to her: "Only one British labourer had, at this time, entered Ningpo—a female, Miss Aldersey, who, with her own independent resources, has been making a praiseworthy effort to impart a Christian education to about twenty female children. The prejudices and suspicions of the parents had been gradually allayed by her judicious and kind management, and their confidence in her was daily increasing. A little babe, rescued from slow starvation, had just been received on the day of my arrival." The Rev. W. Milne, writing to ask help for Miss Aldersey's work, which had grown beyond her means to sustain, speaks of her as "a self-denying, heroic labourer." "The success," he says, "which has already (in 1845) attended her good work in the city of Ningpo, with its 250,000 inhabitants, has surpassed our most sanguine expectations." One story shall be given as a sample of this success. When Miss Aldersey began her work, she was constantly distressed by the piteous cries of a little girl. On inquiry she found that these cries came from a child betrothed to the grandson of the woman who in part owned the house in which she lived. It was only one of many cases she met with, exhibiting the proverbial wretchedness of a child sent into the family of her future husband. Miss Aldersey was told that the girl was so wicked that she required constant beating. One day matters culminated in the poor thing determining to take poison, and trying to persuade a little friend to do the same. Miss Aldersey then urged the woman to give up the child, promising to try her method of reformation. With much difficulty, and after many efforts she succeeded, and no little trouble attended the task. Every day came the assurance that nothing could subdue her but stripes. For a long time the issue seemed doubtful, but love ultimately prevailed. The efforts of Miss Aldersey, aided as they were by those of her adopted daughter, Mary Leisk, and her young native converts, Ati and Kit, all of whom had followed their beloved friend to Ningpo, proved, by God's blessing, effectual.

Miss Leisk was rejoiced one morning, on hearing the voice of prayer, to find a little band was assembled in a private room, and the devotions led by the once hardened child. Better still, her future mother-in-law, who had declared that her hatred of the child was so great that she never addressed her but by some opprobrious name, came to the school to express her delight and surprise at the change in the girl's whole conduct and deportment.

The story of these two young girls, Ati and Kit, is quite a romance. On Miss Aldersey's removal, they were deprived of all religious instruction, and left to the care of persons who took little heed of them. They resolved to follow her, and to perform the journey as correctly as possible, one, the best-looking and most attractive, assumed the name of "the young lady," while the other performed the office of servant or attendant, and in this way they reached the northern portion of the island of Java, from whence they embarked for Ningpo, and arrived safely at the new home of their astonished teacher. They both, years after, married Christian Chinamen, and were made very useful.

About the same time that Ati and Kit were led to give up idolatry and avouch themselves Christians, Chunncô and Hancô in Singapore took the same step. They were known to Ati, and a letter written in her own hand in English to the committee in England will give a stronger proof of the elevating influence of Christian instruction than any words from others.

"NINGPO, 16*th April*, 1846.

"RESPECTED LADIES,—I hope you will excuse me in writing to you. We are so thankful, and praise God for His great goodness to us, in that He has made known His blessed Gospel, and has put in the hearts of His good people to pity us, and some have left their comforts and beloved friends behind, to go so far to teach the ignorant and perishing heathen. We are very much interested in Chunnô and Hancô. We knew them both before they were converted. When we had news from them that they had become the disciples of Jesus, it astonished me very much. It was as news from heaven, for we were so lonely, because there were none of our sex who were Christians which we knew besides us two, my companion and I. . . . Though we are far from each other, we can comfort each other with letters. As we were heathen formerly, we can sympathise with them. We are very anxious about our parents, for they have no hope. I can only pray, but I hope the Almighty God will hear my prayers for them. . . . Pardon the errors of this letter; finally, pray for us, that we may grow in grace and in the knowledge of our Lord and Saviour Jesus Christ.—I am yours respectfully,

"RUTH ATI."

In perusing the journals and letters of Miss Aldersay, extending as they do over a period of twenty-three years, the one difficulty is to make a selection. For some time she was regarded as a female cannibal, and tales were told that she picked out the eyes of some of the children, while she ate others. For a short time it was generally believed that she had murdered all the children who had gone to her house. She was a very early riser, and took her morning walk about four o'clock. To account for this habit, the Chinese said she went thus early to hold intercourse with the evil spirits of the night, and that she might drink the blood of the children she killed.

One letter tells of an attempt to teach a poor blind woman, who, having heard something of the Gospel from a native Christian, Sing-a-foh, came to hear the way of God explained more fully. Her family took alarm, a mob assembled round the "barbarian white woman's" house, threw stones, and were so violent that Miss Aldersey had to retreat to a boat for safety. Soon after, she was cheered by no less than eighty women from another city coming to visit her. It was a day on which they were going to the temple to give rice to the priests, and buy bills on the bank of heaven. This means that they give pieces of cash for some bits of printed paper, which being preserved till death, are then burned, in the belief that they will be available in Hades.

About the same time, a letter arrived from one of

her girls married in a distant village, saying she was teaching eight girls "the doctrine," adding "ask God to show me how, and to give me a Christian spirit. We have begun family prayer." Another girl, Sing Asan, dying with disease in the chest, unable to lie down, was patiently looking forward in perfect peace to her home in heaven, "praying only," she said, "to the true God."

We might fill pages with accounts of Miss Aldersey's self-denying work among female opium-eaters. One Chinese lady whom she took into her own house, and had to watch by night as well as by day, was induced to abandon the habit after many relapses, and there was reason to believe became a true Christian. Miss Aldersey naïvely says: "I told her at once she must destroy her pipe; she is to bring her guitar, and she and Mary Leisk are to try their skill together. Truly it is no joke to have such a guest, but as she seems in earnest, I invited her to come and go through the painful weaning under my eye. She has been in the habit of rising in the middle of the night and calling some one up to prepare a meal. Her habits are an annoyance to Europeans, but when I think of the possibility of her receiving the Gospel, all such little matters appear nothing to me. She is astonished at all she sees and hears."

A short account of two of the brightest amongst her young converts must conclude this sketch. San Avong, an interesting little girl, was the child of a woman who came to Miss Aldersey as servant. The pay from "the foreign devil" was doubtless the inducement, and as it suited her convenience she consented to the child living with her and being taught. The girl, already betrothed, was soon married, and shortly became a widow, when she returned to her English friend. The truth had taken hold of her heart, and she became Miss Aldersey's faithful friend and helper. She prayed much for her mother and other relatives, and earnestly besought them to come and learn the "good doctrine" from her beloved teacher. Miss Aldersey gives the following amusing account of one such interview. "San Avong one day brought a rich female relative, whom she had great difficulty in inducing to come, because of the reports abroad concerning me. The lady was evidently ill at ease. She sat, however, pretty quietly, till I had occasion to put my hand in a bag for the key of a closet where I kept biscuits, and which I wished her to partake of. She then immediately arose, fearing I was drawing out a knife." She could not be persuaded to stay, and excused herself from tasting anything, from the fear of being poisoned. The missionaries used to say that Miss Aldersey was the most notorious person in all Ningpo. God's blessing rested in a remarkable way upon the young missionary's efforts. One day, San Avong found a schoolfellow weeping bitterly, saying she was a great sinner, and soon she and others were led to believe in the one Saviour who died for the sins of the world. As our young widow grew older she increased in knowledge as well as in grace, and opportunities for usefulness opened out before her. She and the Christian girls established a working party, and sold stockings, table mats, and other articles which they made, to pay for the education of some heathen child. On one occasion, San Avong visited a nunnery, and while the inmates were eating rice, told them of "our holy religion." She wrote to Miss Aldersey: "One woman seemed quite interested. She urged us to take tea and tiffin. I am quite surprised at her kindness. On Saturday, many more desired to hear of our doctrine. While speaking, I prayed that I might be faithful. We read the Scriptures to them, and some asked, 'How must we worship Jesus?'" The two young converts who accompanied her could not talk to their fellow-countrywomen as she did, but, they simply said, they stood by and prayed. Another time our young widow went to a hospital, built outside the city, for the blind and disabled. It is one of the very few places supported by Chinese charity. The poor inmates, numbering several hundreds, thought some bad motive must have actuated their visitors. But San Avong told them of the love of Jesus, and induced a few children to take their first lesson in the art of reading. The increasing usefulness of this young evangelist led Miss Aldersey, whose infirmities and age were unfitting her for the constant work of past years, to seek a protection for her. After a formal proposal from Yi Loh Ding, they were betrothed, and soon after married. This young man had been a heathen opium-smoker, but was now not only a Christian, but a preacher of the Gospel. They soon began to itinerate in the towns and villages, and while he spoke to the men, San Avong went from house to house among the women.

In the midst of her usefulness, this young Christian was suddenly called home. While all were mourning around her, she told them "she was very happy." She committed her new-born baby to the care of Miss Aldersey, and when her husband, in an agony of grief, exclaimed, "O San Avong, what shall I do without you?" she replied, "Don't rest on *me*. Go to Jesus. He will never fail you. *He* is with me now. He sustains and blesses me." And in this happy state of mind she fell asleep. The God whom she had loved and served for ten years was with her in the valley of death, and to the last she kept repeating promises out of His Word. May not English Christians say: "Let my last end be like hers?"

Another of our friend's valued helpers was Agnes Gutzlaff, a blind girl. This dear young woman became a very decided Christian, and had the benefit of several years' teaching in England. After Miss Aldersay gave up school teaching, Agnes carried on much of her work, and was invaluable among the blind, who, alas! abound in China. She also assisted in visiting the native Christian families. One blind woman with her two children resided on the mission premises. A blind pupil who had given Agnes much sorrow by her bad behaviour became thoroughly changed by God's blessing upon her teacher's long-suffering and patience, and only returned home that she might try and lead her relatives to that Saviour whom she had found to be so precious.

Among the many who were led to seek the Saviour through the instrumentality of Miss Aldersey and her native and other helpers was an old lady aged eighty.

She gave the strongest testimony to the reality of the change that a Chinese could do. As the result of many years' hard earnings, she had purchased a large collection of *kewan-dea*. These are regarded as a sort of bills on the bank of Hades, of which (so say the priests) the newly deceased person will get the benefit on arriving in the world of spirits. After her conversion the old lady publicly burned these bills herself amidst the expressed horror and astonishment of the bystanders. When she ended by throwing the dust of the burnt papers into the river, the people groaned out their wailing lamentation over the unheard-of loss, and the fearful abuse of such sacred things.

In 1857, Miss Aldersey, after resigning the school in Ningpo, joined some relatives in Australia, where, in a good old age, and active to the last in her Lord's service, she was called to her heavenly rest. "The memory of the just is blessed."

Miss Harriet Baxter, in like manner, devoted her life and fortune to China's women, and only the great day will reveal fully the blessing resulting from the work of these labourers. Since their removal much has been done in the way of female education in that vast empire. Mrs. Smith, wife of the then Bishop of Victoria, opened day schools, in which the old obstacle arose of the children being in danger of being kidnapped on their way to and fro; and where the injunction given to the teacher by the mother of one of the first pupils was to be sure and beat her well. But by degrees obstacles were overcome, and at the present time there are in China over a hundred lady missionaries, besides missionaries' wives.

Great blessing has attended the efforts of the converts to lead their fellow-countrywomen to Christ. A missionary, lately, on visiting a distant village, was surprised by a number of women coming and begging him to baptise them. On inquiry, he was told that the village had been visited by an old resident who had returned to see her relations. That she told her friends all about "the doctrine"; read out of the white foreigners' Book, and told them of the peace and happiness of believing in Jesus. As a result, many of the women had become believers, burnt their ancestral tables, and assembled together to read and pray, and now a missionary had come they besought him to baptise them into the faith of Christ.

The late Mrs. Edkins, of the London Missionary Society, possessed a marvellous knowledge of the Chinese language, and for many years was pre-eminently useful in establishing schools and Bible classes for the women, many of whom died rejoicing in their new-found Saviour, who would doubtless welcome her into her heavenly home. One of the converts came to her lady friend weeping and in sore distress. Her heathen husband had got himself involved in debt, and to meet it had just proposed to sell his little daughter, a mere child, to a Chinaman, twenty years her senior. English mothers can enter into the feelings of this poor native in the prospect of having her little one thus snatched from her, and taken where she might never see or hear of her again. The result of the efforts made in behalf of this poor child were never known.

The missionary tours of Mrs. Gulick, formerly Miss De la Cour, of the Female Education Society, would fill a volume. Their mode of travelling was this. Mr. Gulick on his horse, mounted on bedding and saddle-bags, containing a month's supply of clothes, books, and medicines. His wife on her white donkey, Donny, with provision bags hanging to her saddle. The days passed happily in curing the sick, and pointing all with whom they came into contact to the Saviour. The nights were trying, but she wrote: "We get used to brick beds, dirt, torn windows, and nightly attacks from four or five different tribes of a liliputian army. I was amused, when putting the bridle on Donny, to hear a bystander exclaim, 'Ah, none of our women could do that; they only know how to drink tea.'" At night stones would sometimes be thrown into their place of rest, with the hope that they might go out to scold, and thus some who had not done so before would get a sight of the "white foreign devil."

In addition to teaching, the work done by many missionary ladies in translating is considerable. Miss Oclad, a labourer of twenty years' standing, translated into Chinese the first hymn book used by the Church in that land. She has since translated Mr. Eugene Stock's "Steps to Truth" into Japanese.

The need of more labourers is great. Infanticide still prevails to an awful extent. One woman recently acknowledged to a Bible-woman that she had with her own hands killed fourteen children.

CHAPTER X.

BURMAH.

"Fellow helpers to the truth."—3 John 8.

T O American ladies belongs the honour of commencing female education in the East. They were the pioneers in this good work, which they began in the first year of this century. Two years later the Massachusetts Baptist Missionary Society was formed, out of which sprang "The Female Mite," "Female Cent," and other ladies' societies. In 1819, the Female Missionary Society of the Methodist Episcopal Church was formed.

Little is recorded of woman's work in Burmah till 1822, when Mrs. Judson, who, with her husband, had been toiling at the language since 1813, returning to America for the restoration of her health, pictured in burning words the condition of women without Christ in India and Burmah. She besought her Christian sisters to lay aside superfluous luxuries and ornaments in the house and on the person, and to devote their price to carry out the work of God abroad.

On her return to Burmah in 1824, her husband, by invitation of the King, settled in Ava the capital, where she at once began a school with three little girls. But the war broke out, and was followed by the dreadful sufferings so graphically described in the lives of these devoted people. As soon as they were set at liberty, they settled at Amherst, where Mrs. Judson again opened a school. But family cares soon partially stopped the work, and requests were sent to America for unmarried ladies. Four only were at that time allowed to engage in the mission, as the officials at home wrote that, " they did not feel sufficiently sure that single women would be brave, and steady, and contented, when far from home and relatives, and at the same time prudent as to their health, and willing to be guided." Mrs. Carpenter, herself sorely needing such help, seems to have had a better opinion of her sisters at home. Writing about the matter some years later, she says, "As yet we have no helper ; our signal of distress is raised : our cry for help repeated again and again, but so far none respond." Helpers did, however, come, though it was remarkable that the very day one of them first met the committee, a fire broke out, which burned up the city, and the outfit prepared for her was consumed in the depot. Timely aid was given, funds were provided, and she sailed at the appointed time for her eastern home. Many were the difficulties to be encountered, but, as one of her countrywomen wrote: " When did a woman with a Divine instinct within her fail, because of incredulity or indifference?" Since Mary broke her alabaster box, she has met, and triumphed over such, and won the encomium of her Lord. "When seeking to trace some of the secrets of the success God has granted, we have at least found one. These dollars have come with a value not recognised in the commercial markets, memoirs of the departed, the hard earnings and close savings of the living, baptised in heart-blood, and consecrated with prayer." A lady from Ohio, having been used by God at home, and accepted for foreign work, was waiting till sufficient money was raised to send her, when a woman's meeting was held to deliberate on the steps to be taken. One of their number arose exclaiming, "And shall we lose her because we have not the needed money in our hands? No! rather let us resolve to walk the streets of Boston in calico robes, and save the expense of more costly apparel. I move Miss T——'s appointment to India." The response of all present, only twenty in number, was "We will send her." There are now no less than twenty distinct female missionary societies in America, but as numbers and statistics do not possess the interest of facts, the little space left shall contain a sketch of a few of the gifted and saintly women thus sent, and the marvellous blessing that rested upon their labours. Perhaps the work among the Burmans and Karens is more striking than any others in the whole range of modern missions.

It was on the 19th of February, 1812, that the brig weighed anchor which was to convey Mr. and Mrs. Judson and their fellow-workers to the land of their adoption. Of that devoted band, they alone were permitted to land in Rangoon. Ere long, a small, low, thatched building called a zayat was built by the way-side, on the road leading to the Great Pagoda, and here day by day did they, first through an interpreter, and then with loosened tongue, proclaim the message of salvation to the crowds that were constantly passing. Here Mrs. Judson opened her first girls' school; here she assembled the women, and told them of the woman's Saviour. Here it was that, when the war with England broke out, she, with the other missionaries and their wives, were arrested, laden with heavy chains, and hurried off to the common prison. In vain they urged that they were Americans, and had no connection with the British Government. Here it was that fifty Burmans entered their prison, took off their outer garments, and drove them to the place of execution. Here, when she, Mrs. Hough, and Mrs. Wade were rescued by British officers, did this noble woman by her earnest appeals to the Governor obtain permission to erect a little bamboo hut within the precincts of the prison yard in which the missionaries were immured, and for nine weary months prepared their food, ministered to their wants, and, as opportunity offered, whispered of a Saviour's love to the degraded native women with whom she was daily brought into contact.

Shortly after, the approach of the British army to the capital alarmed the King, who then commanded the services of Dr. Judson as part of an embassy to the English camp, with overtures of peace. On the conclusion of peace the missionaries were set free. Friends were not wanting who urged the released captives, after two years of almost unparalleled suffering, to return, and rest, at least, for awhile in their native land. But their hearts were set upon winning the Burmese to Christ. Amherst was fixed upon as the future capital of the English possessions in Burmah, and here Dr. and Mrs. Judson once more unfurled the standard of the cross under the strong arm of British protection. Hardly were her schools opened when Mrs. Judson, whose constitution never recovered the shock it had sustained, sunk under an attack of fever. She and the little daughter, born during their captivity, were buried at Amherst, thus taking possession of the soil for Christ. Never was that text more fulfilled, she "being dead yet speaketh." A catechism which she had written was now put into the hands of the children who could no longer hear the living voice, and through it many were led to read God's Word, and were made wise unto salvation.

While the good work was thus proceeding at Rangoon, Mrs. Wade, Mrs. Mason, and Mrs. Boardman were toiling among the women of Tavoy. This city was the stronghold of Buddhism, and at that time numbered 200 priests and upwards of 2000 pagodas. "Here," writes the latter, "we are gathering some of the dear scattered lambs of the fold. The room for Mr. Boardman, myself, and our little boy to live in is not above five feet wide and ten feet long, and so low that I cannot stand upright in it." From this lowly home Mr. Boardman, worn out with toil, was called to his heavenly rest. His widow resolved not to abandon her beloved work. She wrote, "The superintendence of the boarding and the village schools, with food and clothing for the girls in the former, and five day schools devolves wholly on me."

At the end of three years of widowhood, Mrs. Boardman married Dr. Judson, leaving behind her in Tavoy Mrs. Mason, a fellow-worker, to carry on her schools, every way fitted to follow in her steps. Mrs. Judson perfected her knowledge of Burmese, and made great proficiency in the Karen language. She assisted Dr. Judson in his translation of the entire Scriptures into Burman,—a laborious work, often under the pressure of severe bodily suffering. On the 31st January, 1834, we find this touching entry in his handwriting: "Thanks be to God, I can now say I have attained. I have knelt down before Him with the last leaf in my hand, and imploring His forgiveness for all the sins which have polluted my labours, and His aid in future efforts to remove the errors and imperfections which cleave to the work. I have commended it to His mercy, and dedicated it to His glory."

Mrs. Judson now became interested in many women and children of the Peguan race, who were numerous in the neighbourhood of Maulmein, though quite distinct from the Burmans and Karens. The Judsons were residing on British territory, but became acquainted with these Peguans living across the border, over whom our representative had no control. With great labour she learned their language, and translated into it a considerable portion of the New Testament, a task which no other member of the mission was then able to accomplish. The Word of God, accompanied by the power of the Holy Ghost, now wrought a great change in the people, and hundreds embraced "the new doctrine." Nor was it long before their fidelity to it was to be tested. A violent persecution arose. A royal command was issued to exterminate the white people and the foreign religion. The Karen Christians were hunted from place to place; whole families were seized and cruelly beaten, while Christian mothers, separated from their children, were driven like sheep to prison.

Captain Phayre, the assistant commissioner, was indeed a Good Samaritan. He supplied many with food, and advanced loans without interest. Hundreds left their homes and fled across the mountains into Arracan. Here they were cared for by their American friends. Mr. and Mrs. Comstick settled in their midst, where the latter began to teach the women and girls. In the midst of her labours she was seized with cholera, and the following year her husband sank under the same disease. His memorable message to the Churches at home was not forgotten, "Remember, brother, six men for Arracan." His dying words were thus paraphrased:—

> "Tell them that near yon idol dome,
>   There dwells a lonely man,
> Who bade you take this message home,
>   Six men for Arracan.
>
> Well, in those lovely scenes of bliss,
>   Where childhood's joys began,
> I'd have you, brother, tell them this,
>   Six men for Arracan."
>
> Yon dying saint, he lingers yet,
>   And casts one thought on man;
> "Be this the last that you forget,
>   Six men for Arracan."

Meantime Dr. Judson's second wife, whose zeal equalled that of her predecessor, laboured on in Maulmein. She wrote hymns, and translated many books in Burmese, amongst others "The Pilgrim's Progress." In a letter home she said, "It would do your heart good to see our praying women; so humble, so devout, so willing to confess their faults to God, and before one another. I sometimes think Christians at home might well copy them. The Bible class increases. One woman upwards of seventy told me a few days ago, she was the same age as my little daughter Abby. When I asked what she meant, she said she was converted the year Abby was born, and it was not till then that she began to live." One convert in dying reached out the only rupee she possessed, exclaiming, "Teacher, take this for the building of a chapel."

Another American lady, Mrs. Ingolls, who left her home as a bride to labour in Burmah, and as wife and widow continues in her beloved work, must be mentioned, though space forbids us giving details. Amid a company of women whom she had been instrumental in leading to Jesus, was one aged woman, who shortly before her death exclaimed, "Let the king of death now come. I am ready to depart to my Lord. I have confessed His holy name."

Meanwhile Mrs. Mason was carrying on her work in Tavoy. From the beginning of her career she accompanied her husband in his dangerous jungle tours, where she gathered the women around her, and told the ever new story of a Saviour's love. As her Karen girls left the schools in the town for homes of their own in the mountains, they produced a great impression by their altered habits and conduct. In one sequestered glen there lived a former pupil, named Naughapo. She became the Dorcas of the neighbourhood, feeding the hungry, soothing the afflicted, and making her little dwelling the home of many little ones, that they might go to the school and hear of Jesus. On one occasion Mrs. Mason expressed her admiration of her peaceful lovely home, when she replied, "We neither of us think that it or anything we have is our own. All, all is God's." The day before Mrs. Mason left her, a box wallah called with his tempting fabrics for sale. It was but rarely such an opportunity offered in that distant place to make a purchase. But, though Naughapo was in very poor garments, she spent but one rupee, and on the following morning put thirteen into her beloved teacher's hand to deposit in the mission treasury.

Such were some of the fruits of Helen Mason's teaching. She had asked God to give her the souls of all the pupils in her first Karen school, and what she asked she obtained, though it was ten years before the last confessed her faith in Christ. From her six day schools, one and another as they grew to womanhood came asking to be allowed "to read Jesus Christ's books" to their heathen neighbours. For five long years not one single soul in Mergui or Tavoy became a convert; now fruit was abounding to the joy of her heart. One and then another and another woman came forward to assist in this labour of love. But the labour of years was telling upon this prematurely old worker. She would half playfully say, "I shall vanish away from you before long." She prepared clothes for her children, and arranged all in her home.

In the little mission cemetery near her house there was a small bamboo oratory, fitted with a chair, table, and Bible, in which the saintly Boardman was said "to have prayed the Karen Mission into existence." To this retreat Helen Mason often retired, and would spend hours in fasting and prayer, communing with God, and feeding on angels' food. Her strength grew gradually less. There was no disease, it was simply exhaustion. From the beginning to the end she had perfect peace. "Tell the native Christians," she said, "that I loved them to the end, and had it been the will of God, I would have gladly stopped and taught them longer. My peace has been like a river. The words of my Saviour have been verified to me: 'My peace I give unto you.'" She was eminently a woman of prayer. Her husband wrote: "Often, times without number, have I awoke in the silent watches of the night, and found that she had stolen from my side, and was holding earnest communion with God." This, doubtless, was the secret of her success. In one of her last letters she says: "Pray much and often for me that I may 'Abide in Christ,' 'Live in the Spirit and walk in the Spirit;'" and in this frame of mind she entered upon her heavenly rest.

Great political changes took place in Burmah in 1852. An official letter ran thus:—"20th December, 1852.—To-day the solemn act of dismembering the Burman empire took place on board her Britannic

Majesty's ship *Fox*. The proclamation declaring the incorporation of the ancient kingdom of Pegu in the empire of British India, was publicly read, and a royal salute fired in honour of the event." This annexation included the district of Bassein, and united in one continuous sea-board Pegu, Arracan, and Tenasserim. It was in the jungles of these places that Mrs. Mason first sought out the girls, whom she induced for a time to leave their Karen villages and come to her schools at Tavoy. Many of the Sho children also became her pupils.

The annexation of three millions of people from what has well been called "the most heartless and oppressive Government in all Asia" opened a wide field for unmolested evangelistic labour. Soon zayats, or houses for prayer, were erected along the whole line of the river to the Huckang Valley. "There," wrote Dr. Mason, " we can stand on the borders of Western China, and on the upper waters of the Great Cambodea, and reach by books and teaching untold millions."

Mrs. Mason (Dr. Mason's second wife) threw her whole soul into the work, and before three years and a-half had elapsed hundreds of women and children could read God's Word in their own tongue. "Three years ago," she writes, "they came in troops, wild mountaineers, with their short striped gowns and unwashed faces; now all are neatly dressed in clean new gowns, and their hair neatly braided. I could not but exclaim, 'What hath God wrought!'"

Not satisfied with these results, Mrs. Mason resolved to commence a native self-supporting Female Education Society. As the Mission had not funds available for such an establishment, she determined to appeal to English and American friends and to the people themselves. She drew out her plans, explained and showed them to the natives, and received from them one hundred " pledge letters " of support, accompanied by "blessings on the teacheress for ever." Government gave her the land and 1400 rupees. "It is true," she wrote, "the land is only an unbroken jungle, and every one says I shall lose my life in clearing it. But, knowing that fearless soldiers must have fearless leaders, I pitched my tent in the wilderness, and took my schools with me. There we fed those who came down to clear the land, and who poured down from the hills to the number of 200 for many days together. One of the early converts, Shapan, now an evangelist, naïvely remarked: 'The women worked hard, but the men were very idle.'"

While Mrs. Mason was thus working in the jungle her pen was not idle, and among those to whom she wrote, and who warmly responded to her appeal, were the ladies forming the committee of the Female Education Society in London. To them she wrote as follows:—" I established this school on an entirely different principle from that of any institution in India. All the land, buildings, apparatus, furniture, books—everything—I give unreservedly to the people. It is not to be the property of any foreign society. The pupils are to enter at twelve, none for less than a year, and the people are to support them entirely, besides keeping the buildings in repair and the land in order." The Rev. W. Hazeldine, chaplain in the East

Indian Company's service, having seen the work, confirmed Mrs. Mason's statements, and said, "There seemed a Pentecostal outpouring of the Spirit now in Burmah."

The society largely helped her work, while presents of books, globes, maps, and even a piano, were sent for the new school. From her interesting little book, "Tounghoo Women," we extract the following:—"A few years ago, not a Karen woman in this region could read a syllable, now hundreds can, and fifty are already training as teachers to their countrywomen. Even the robber chiefs are asking to have them sent into their districts. We want them both as school teachers and Bible-women. Already six Christian villages on one range, and fifteen on the north, have been raised up as if by magic from the darkness of heathenism. Like the prophet in the vision, we are overwhelmed with the scenes passing before our eyes. There is no doubt here whether the Bible shall be taught in their schools. We are welcomed as 'the white teachers who bring the Book.' If you would have Burmah redeemed to the Lord, send women to women. Let them teach the A B C of Christianity, which is mother's work all the world over. One of our women, speaking of a missionary for whom they entertained the most profound esteem, said, 'He is like Mount Meru—very high. He knows everything. But he can't talk women's talk, and we don't understand.' Now, if it be supposed by any good society that we aim to supersede, or in any way to interfere with men's work at all, we can only say, they are utterly mistaken. *They don't understand.* Let them come and see."

In another letter Mrs. Mason writes that she had a visit from a Burmese lady of rank anxious to see her schools and hear of "the doctrine." "She was sixty-five years of age, a former Governor's wife, and had seven or eight ladies in her suite. Her fingers were gemmed with the nine magic stones of Burmah. Having ordered mats, I took a low seat by my visitors and inquired if the lady wished to hear of Jesus Christ. 'I have come to hear,' was the answer. 'I have lived sixty-five years.' 'Indeed! then the great mother is as old as my grandmother. I am but a child beside her. Nevertheless God in great mercy has shown me the true way to happiness.' 'Let us hear! let us hear!' exclaimed the attendants. So I tried to tell them slowly and solemnly of man's sinful state; of his need of a Saviour; of that Saviour offered, and the peace that comes on receiving Him. On my saying that she would perhaps be grieved when I told her that God was displeased when people worshipped idols, she replied, 'You are a woman the same as myself, only you have more knowledge. The words you speak are not your own, they are God's words. We must receive them as God's words!' The great stumbling-block in the way of their receiving Jesus is, that they have been all their lives (like some in Christian countries) laying up merit of their own wherewith to earn heaven. 'You think it hard,' I said, 'to give up what you call merit.' 'Yes, madam, I have done much in my lifetime for pagodas and monasteries. It is hard, very hard!' In this way I have sat from eight o'clock till four, day by day for weeks together, sometimes having forty visitors a-day. The body would often weary; the spirit never. There are in Burmah at least three millions of women. If these are christianised Burmah will be christianised. Woman is the educator of Burmah, and, strange to say, she carries on much of the business and trade of the country. It is she who teaches the toddling child to tug its dress full of sand every night to the pagoda. She it is also who excites discord, fans rebellion, and overturns dynasties. She *can*, and she *will* rise. Teach her to rise towards God, and let us do it ere it is too late. 'Don't tell me,' exclaimed one aged woman, 'I am too old. I can't learn your prayer. Your Jesus doesn't know me. I've fed the priests. If I take another religion now I shall fall between the two. Let me alone. If I'm lost, I'm lost. Had I heard when I was young I might have believed, but now too late, too late.'" A later letter tells of much blessing. "Guapung, a female converted to Christianity before Mrs. Mason went to Burmah, had been the means of leading her husband, and all her family, and many around her to Christ. Her life was so holy and consistent. She treasured up and repeated the Scriptures in a wonderful way, till she was the means of raising up three native village churches. 'She often accompanied me,' says Mrs. Mason, 'in my visits to the women, I reading the Bible, she talking it.' Before her conversion she had been a fortune-teller. One day, a woman who had not heard of the change in her, came five miles to get a charm for her husband, who had run away from her. 'Yes,' said Guapung, 'I have a charm. Sit down sister.' So down she sat, and listened the whole day to the story of Jesus and His love. 'This wonderful Being, who came down to this world, one day saw a woman crying. He went up to her and said, "Why weepest thou, Mary?" Then He spoke kind words to her, and made her happy. Now this wonderful Being who spoke so kindly to a woman was the Son of God.' Then she told the woman the charm was to go and tell her husband, and when he came back never to scold him more, as the Son of God commanded women to obey their husbands.'

"Three weeks after this conversation, a man came over from a heathen village asking to see 'the big teacheress that had the charm.' He added, 'that the woman who had been such a brawler that nobody could live in peace in the neighbourhood was then living very happily with her husband, the quietest of them all. And the men of the place wanted all their wives to join the Christians, as their religion did not allow women to scold their husbands.'"

In one of Mrs. Mason's last letters, alluding to her Institute, she said: "I never saw brighter or more hopeful scholars. We had to send some girls back to the jungle for want of room, as it is limited to fifty pupils. Their studies embrace reading, writing, geography, history, something of natural philosophy, physiology, and the Holy Scriptures; also sewing, cooking, washing, and general cleanliness, nursing the sick and training children. The Karens have lately resolved to adopt a national banner, and their chief native pastor, San Quala, wrote asking the American Bible Society to furnish them with one. A writer in the 'New York World' remarks: 'This strange, wild people (the Karens) are being rapidly christianised, and have sent to America for a national flag to commemorate their exodus out of heathenism! the most curious and exhilarating request that we ever heard of from a new nation.' 'The national banner we choose,' says San Quala, 'is not a lion or any beast, but the weapon which God has given us by which to subdue our enemies, even "The Word of God, which is the sword of the Spirit." It is beautifully got up; the motto is in the Karen language in large white letters, and the flag is on a blue ground with the device of a Bible and a sword in colours.'"

This sketch of the work of our noble American sisters must not be concluded without some reference to their labours amongst the Eurasians of Burmah.

It is now more than forty years since a missionary, living in one of the small cities of British Burmah, left his study with a heavy heart and strolled out for an evening walk. He had not gone far when he met two girls attired in English costume, which at that early period of British occupation was so rare that it attracted his attention.

Seeing them at nightfall in a heathen city without protection, he stopped and accosted them, when with full hearts they told their sorrowful tale.

They were children of a European father and a heathen Burmese mother. From domestic causes, which the missionary subsequently found to be true, they had been turned out of doors, exposed to temptations from which their unknown heavenly Father rescued them through this unlooked-for meeting. From them he and his wife heard much of the condition of

Eurasian girls in similar circumstances, and they at once resolved to give them a home and Christian training. Hardly had these girls become domiciled with the American missionary and his wife, when passing the street he saw a pretty fair child, bearing unmistakable signs of European extraction — brown hair and blue eyes. On inquiry he was told that she was the daughter of an English officer who had been lawfully married to a native wife, but had died some years before, without having been able to make any provision for the little one.

Left thus entirely to the care of Burman relatives, she had been brought up in idolatry, and had from infancy been taught to bow before gods of wood and stone. The missionary's wife soon made an effort to secure her as fellow-pupil, and consent was given that she should come every day. Thus was formed the nucleus of the first Burmese Eurasian school.

One day, months after, there was a heathen festival, and she was told that she must accompany her mother to the pagoda. How great was that mother's astonishment when the child tremblingly told her that she never could pray to an idol again. To her mother's questions, Phœbe replied that there was but one God—the great God who made the world and all that was in it; who had sent His only begotten Son, Jesus, to die for sinners, and that she loved Him, for He had forgiven her all her sins and made her happy. Horrified at the child's heresy, the angry mother thrust her out of the house, telling her she should never enter it again. The child at once sought refuge at the mission-house, where she met with a cordial welcome.

For a long time every effort to see her mother proved fruitless. But one day Phœbe was told that her mother was very ill, and overcoming all obstacles she crept to her side. But no mother's love welcomed her. When able to speak, she upbraided her in harsh words for forsaking her mother's religion. Every effort to lead her to Jesus seemed in vain. Day and night during her long illness did the daughter tenderly watch over and nurse her, receiving nothing but unkindness in return. As the end approached she asked to be raised, and feebly clasping her hands in adoration before the idol opposite to her bed she expired. That terrible death-bed scene gave a tone to all Phœbe's after life, and she solemnly resolved to do all that lay in her power to lead her heathen sisters to Christ.

The seed sown was not lost. All three girls, and others who came afterwards, proved by their lives that they were true Christians. All married and had happy Christian homes. The children of one of them have been educated in England, and are both now missionaries in their native land. Phœbe became the wife of a native minister, and her son is now preaching Christ in Burmah.

But this is not all. Many years ago an American lady opened a mission school for Burmese girls, when Phœbe offered her help, which was gladly accepted.

This school has been greatly blessed. Not only has it one hundred boarders, but in connection with it are five day schools in the city, and others in the jungle villages.

Many of the pupils, through the influence of this Eurasian woman, have been led to confess Christ.

Having some Asiatic blood, she came closer to them than a foreigner possibly could.

For a time, owing to deaths and removals, this school was discontinued. But one day Miss Haswell, who was labouring diligently amongst the Burmese, was entreated by a native Christian woman to rescue a Eurasian girl who had that day been sold by her heathen mother for the sum of £30. Immediate action was taken, the law interfered, and the child was soon sheltered in the mission home. Hearing that one Eurasian girl had been taken, the lady missionary was soon beset by applications from others. As these children spoke the English language as well as the native, and generally wore English dress, they could not be taught with the Burmese. Just at that crisis an American lady, who has since visited England, and become well known in many circles, arrived in Burmah, with the intention of relieving Miss Haswell in her arduous work among the natives.

As some time must necessarily elapse ere she could acquire the language, she proposed to devote some hours daily to these Eurasian girls. Her heart was drawn towards neglected English-speaking little ones, and after consideration and prayer both ladies agreed that this was the work to which Mrs. Longley was called. It was a great sacrifice that Miss Haswell was making. Her own work had grown far beyond her enfeebled powers, and she was really sinking under it. Now the long prayed for help had arrived, only to leave her. But the Lord's work and will concerning them was the one and only thing to be considered by both these consecrated ladies, and Miss Haswell gladly consented to struggle on that His kingdom might be advanced.

But difficulties of various kinds now arose. The building hitherto occupied had been erected for only a missionary and his wife, and could not decently accommodate the numbers now flocking to enter it. The house stood upon piles; and the earth below was saturated with water from the long-continued rains. There were no windows, and during the high winds and storms the wooden shutters had to be closed, or the rooms would be flooded. The result of the foul air and want of ventilation was an outburst of illness. A deserted room across the compound was substituted, but here the scorching rays of the sun came through the broken roof, and, in addition to other ailments, the devoted teacher was struck with blindness. While able she had written to America begging for help, and just as thus broken down she was ordered to leave, and told permanent loss of sight would ensue, she received an answer saying that lack of funds would prevent the society at home from giving her any help. It was under these touching circumstances that this devoted lady visited England to plead the cause of Eurasian girls. As there is a prejudice in the minds of some with reference to this class, on account of their supposed parentage, it may be well to state that the statistics prove over ninety-six per cent. are born of parents united in lawful wedlock.

CHAPTER XI.

PERSIA.

"It shall come to pass in the latter days, that I will bring again the captivity of Elam, saith the Lord."—Jer. xlix. 39.

HENRY MARTYN'S name is inseparably connected with mission work in Persia, but it was not until many years after his death that Christian women began their labours in that country.

Dr. Fiske, an American missionary, who had laboured many years in the East, when at Mount Holyoke made a request for a young lady to go as missionary teacher to the degraded women of Persia. Fidelia Fiske, his niece, responded in these words: "If counted worthy, I shall be willing to go." She was only three years old when her uncle first sailed for the East, but from the day when his first letter from Persia reached the old home the subject of missions was a constant topic of conversation in her father's family, and the thought, as she grew older, seemed to take possession of her mind that she too might be called to carry the Gospel message to heathen lands.

Her mother's consent was obtained, many difficulties were overcome, and on 1st March, 1843, Miss Fiske accompanied a party of devoted men and their wives, and sailed for her Eastern home.

Oroomiah, for ages the sacred city of the fire-worshippers, was henceforth to be the scene of her labours. Its inhabitants were composed of Nestorians, Jews, and Mohammedans. From a published account of the women, at the time of her arrival, we extract the following statement: "The women in their deep degradation are coarse, passionate, and quarrelsome. You may see a whole village of them in a quarrel, with their hair all loose, while they are throwing stones, brickbats, and spoiled eggs at each other, with almost unearthly shrieks." Their personal condition was such as not to admit of description. They were regarded by the men as drudges and slaves, and were compelled to spend most of their time in out-door labour in the vineyards and fields, carrying not only their heavy implements but their infants. When at night they returned from the field they had to milk the cows, prepare their husbands' supper, and wait till they had finished before partaking themselves.

For husbands to beat their wives often and severely, was an almost universal practice. Women and children as well as men were shockingly profane, and lying was so common that "we all lie," was almost proverbial.

When the missionary party settled in Persia there was but one woman in the city who could read. She was Helena, the sister of the Nestorian patriarch. Her superior rank secured her this accomplishment. The rest were not only ignorant, but perfectly content to remain so. When asked if they would not like to learn to read, the invariable answer was, "I am a woman," or, "I am a girl." "Do you want to make a priest of me?"

In 1838 Mrs. Grant, a lady possessed of rare gifts and graces, had opened a school with four little girls. On Miss Fiske taking over the charge, she found that the good learned in school was soon lost by the impure atmosphere of home. She became anxious to change it into a boarding, or, as she termed it, a home school. But the idea was repugnant to all Nestorian views of propriety, and her missionary friends were hopeless as to its possibility. No one would send their girls as boarders, and even Priest Abraham, the most enlightened of the natives, and one who had become a helper, said with strong feeling, "I could not bear the reproach of having my daughter with you as a boarder."

To secure six girls was now the object of Fidelia's deep solicitude. These gained, she had faith to believe that others would follow. The first Syriac word she learned was "daughter," and as she learned to use the verb To give, her constant request was, "Give me your daughter." The day for re-opening the school arrived, and with it fifteen day pupils. Hours passed, and when coming through the court she saw Mar Yohanan leading two little girls. One was Khance, and the other his little niece Selby, aged seven. She says: "I wept tears of joy over them, as the bishop placed their little hands in mine, saying, 'They are your daughters, no man shall take them from you.'"

Several others came for a few days from curiosity, and then ran away. At length six were brought, but only on the condition that they should lodge in a room with or close to their teacher, and never go out but in her company. It was no pleasant work she had thus undertaken. "You can have no idea of their filth," she writes; "they all lie and steal. Nothing is safe except under lock and key; I cannot keep a pin in my pincushion."

One day, feeling much discouraged, she had recourse to the following expedient. Just before they all passed through her room to the flat roof above where they slept, she put six black pins in her cushion, and stepped out till they had passed. As soon as they had gone, she looked and found the pins were gone too. She then called the girls all back and told them of her loss, but no, not one had seen or taken them. Six pairs of little hands were lifted up as they said: "God knows we have not got them." "I think God knows you have," was her reply, and she then searched each one, but found nothing. She then said: "All kneel down, and we will ask God to show who took them," adding, "He may not see fit to show me now, but He will some time." She prayed, and as they rose from their knees, remembered she had not examined their caps. In the first cap were the six pins carefully concealed. The incident did good. The children looked on the discovery as an answer to prayer, and began to be afraid to steal, when God so exposed their thefts. The girl in whose cap the pins were found became a converted and useful woman.

At first a native teacher taught the children to

read, and, to acquire greater facility, Miss Fiske took her place in the class and read in turn with them. She also made them all new native clothes, instead of the dirty rags they came in. Although it was long before any of the women would attend public worship, she soon got a few to come to her room, when she read and prayed with them. When able to speak fluently, she visited the neighbouring villages, always taking her children and a guard with her, as it was not safe to venture without.

By the time her school had increased to twelve, hostile movements were directed towards it. Orders were given that all who attended the mission, including the girls, should at once leave. "If not," so ran the order, "you shall be excommunicated; your finger-nails shall be torn out: we will hunt you from village to village, and kill you if we can."

"I called them together," wrote Miss Fiske, "and told them the reasons why they were to be sent away. I wept like a child, and they all burst into audible weeping. Oh! the bitterness I now felt! To have to send back these children into a darkness like heathenism." All left, except Priest Abraham's daughter, he insisting on her remaining. A thousand children in the boys' schools were thus scattered. By the end of the year the storm had blown over, when our teacher not only had the joy of welcoming all her pupils back, but they brought eight new ones with them; thus making twenty boarders.

Another year rolled by, and so great was the change effected in her pupils, that parents now brought their daughters in such numbers that it was impossible to receive them. One of the first two scholars, Selby, had become an earnest Christian. She was now fourteen, and had been married the year before to a boy a year younger than herself. At her repeated request, she had been allowed to come each day to the school, and take the place of teacher. Her conversion was followed by that of several others. Several of the girls' mothers also became Christians.

Fidelia writes: "My work is almost as much out of the school now as in it. My health is good, and I am happy in my labours. Poor degraded women have been brought to Jesus. It is a great privilege to labour here; here I hope, if it be my Father's will, to make my grave. From here, with many dear ones in Christ Jesus, to go up to meet the Lord, when the final trump shall sound. As far as we know, the converts are walking as Christians. Great tenderness of conscience was manifested. Sins of which they had not been suspected were confessed; stolen articles were restored. Khance, one of my girls, came to me greatly troubled, saying: 'Do you remember the day, two years ago, when Sawdee's shoes were taken?' I said: 'Yes.' 'You thought a Moslem woman took them, but' (bursting into tears) 'I stole them. I was angry with Sawdee, and threw them down the well, where no one could get them. What shall I do? I know Jesus will not forgive me till I have confessed it to Sawdee. May I go and tell her to-night, and pray with her, and then I will go and work and get money to pay her for the shoes?' She did pay for the shoes, and became a bright and shining light in her dark home. We have many cases like this.

"Sarah was a tall dark-eyed girl of twelve or thirteen when she came to me. She was weak and feeble at the time of her conversion, but she would work for Christ. In March we felt that she must die. But all was peace, death had no terrors for her. The story is too long to tell of all this dear girl said and did during the last months of her short life."

Often was the question put by the other pupils, "Will Sarah's hope continue to the last? Will Jesus really stay by her? Will He come for her?" It seemed as if they would test the Lord's faithfulness by the manner in which He should support their young sister. And their expectation was not disappointed. "Since Sarah died," Miss Fiske says, "the Nestorians have looked upon death as they never did before. Heaven's gates are wider opened to them. It is to them now a blessed reality that Christ comes for His own. Her parents were now Christians, and she went home to die. I saw her almost every day; often with her open Bible, and several women by her side, whom she was seeking to lead to Christ. The beautiful Sabbath sun arose, and I was by Sarah's side. She was very happy. I saw that she was almost home, and told her so. I was obliged to return to my school, but said to her mother, 'Send for me when the Master calls for the dear child, for, if I may not go over Jordan with her to-day, I wish to go with her to the swelling stream.' In the afternoon, realising that she must soon go, she said, 'Call my father.' When reminded that he had gone to preach, she at once said, 'Oh yes, I remember. Don't call him. I can die alone.' She then said, 'Call Miss Fiske.' Then the dying child remembered that it was the hour of our prayer meeting. So beckoning to her sister, she said, 'It is the hour when she prays with my companions. Don't call her. I can die alone.' Then she whispered, 'Mother, raise me, that I may commit my spirit.' She was raised by her mother's strong arm, and on bended knee, with upraised eye, she said, 'Lord Jesus, receive——' Her voice ceased. Prayer was ended, and praise begun. The first to love her Saviour was the first to go home. In my own room I heard footsteps on the stairs. The door opened, and one stood by my side with this message, 'Sarah is asleep.'"

Another girl, named Hannah, soon followed. When arranging their things, and putting away their books for the vacation, she said to one in her class, "Perhaps you will open this. I do not think I shall. When you all come again in the autumn, I trust I shall be in the Saviour's school above." The words were prophetic. Hannah was seized with cholera. She said to her companion Guly, "I am very sick. I shall die soon. Shall we not pray together once more?" They knelt together, and having finished her prayer, Guly said, "Now, Hannah, will you pray?" In a half-audible speech she uttered, "Bless my dear sister, and take me through the dark valley." In answer to her friend's question, she said, "I do not fear to die, and go to Jesus."

In 1847, Miss Rice went out to aid Miss Fiske in her ever-increasing duties. The first public examination was held in 1849, when the scholars passed creditably in ancient and modern Syriac, Bible history, geography, and natural philosophy. They not only made all their own clothing, but earned money by sewing and knitting for charitable objects. A fresh attempt was made by the Persian Government in 1856 again to break up the schools, but God interposed. Miss Fiske appealed to R. W. Stephens, Esq., British Consul at Teheran, and the appeal was successful. She wrote: " The design of the school is so to educate Nestorian girls that they may be better daughters, sisters, wives, and mothers. Unless a great change is wrought in the females here, all the efforts in behalf of the other sex will fail to produce permanent good. Besides the duties of the schoolroom, kitchen, and washroom, the pupils are taught to cut and make their own clothing, but the same hand that skilfully uses the needle is found in summer among the golden wheat, holding the sickle, and in autumn gathering the vintage."

But the time came when it was absolutely necessary that the teacher should return to her American home for the rest so sorely needed. Just before she left Persia she had the joy of seeing four of her earliest pupils, with their husbands, depart as missionaries to the dark mountains of Koordistan. A few days after, ninety-three of these once degraded Nestorians commemorated with her the Saviour's dying love, and there was only one out of the whole number with whom she had not prayed! On the morning of her departure seventy of her pupils asked for one more prayer meeting in the Bethel where so many prayers had been offered and answered.

It proved to be the last. Her strength never rallied sufficiently to allow her to return. Her disease made rapid progress. A few days before her death she said, "As I grow weaker I think less of the pain, and feel more the Saviour's arms about me, and it is sweet to feel them." On the last day of her life, as a friend entered her room, she held out her hand, saying, "Will you pray?" As the prayer ascended, her spirit was caught up to learn the strains of the everlasting song of praise.

"They that be wise shall shine as the brightness of the firmament; and they that turn many to righteousness as the stars for ever and ever."

During their late visit to England, the Rev. Dr. and Mrs. Bruce, who have long toiled in this field, did much to excite an interest in behalf of the women of Persia. As a result, funds were raised, and they have returned to their former sphere of labour in Julfa, accompanied by a young lady sent out by the Society for Promoting Female Education.

May God raise up many a woman to bring "light, and gladness, and joy, and honour," into many a dark Persian home.

CHAPTER XII.

SYRIA, PALESTINE, AND VARIOUS MISSIONS.

" And upon the handmaids in those days will I pour out My Spirit."
JOEL ii. 29.

PASSING notice must now be given of some out of the many other spheres where Christian ladies are working, in the hope that a review of the names will lead many to lift up their hearts to God and implore His blessing upon their labours.

In Japan, "The land of the rising sun," the Sun of righteousness has begun to shine.

That country was only opened to foreigners through the commercial treaties of 1854 and 1858, and in 1859 American messengers of peace were already taking possession of it for the Lord.

Miss M'Lean and other ladies are working among the women. It is interesting to notice the difference between the commencement and the results here and in India. In that country men toiled alone at first with small apparent effect. In Japan, on the contrary, 147 Protestant missionaries, exclusive of their wives, entered, with 46 single ladies. In 1870 there were not 10 native Protestants, now they amount to 5000.

About 1828 the Americans began the labours which have been greatly blessed of God in Turkey. The lady missionaries generally found their Turkish sisters willing to make their acquaintance. They liked to examine the dress of their new friends; and even in Turkish seraglios some have been found who were worshippers of the true God, and knew Him as their own personal Saviour.

Good work has also been done by American missionaries in Greece. On the overthrow of the Turkish power in 1830, Dr. Hill and his wife founded the first schools for both sexes in Athens. Subsequently the Government undertook the boys, when Mrs. Hill had the charge of the girls assigned her by the State, and for more than fifty years has this noble woman spent her life in educating nearly three generations of Greek women. An old Syrian proverb says, "The hand that rocks the cradle moves the world." If this be true, there is a bright hope for the future of Greece, as this matron missionary has literally rocked the cradles and cared for the bodies and souls of more than 500 girls each year for half-a-century. She has been abundantly rewarded in the blessed result of her ministrations. Her training schools have sent teachers throughout Greece, and additional means only are required to add to their number. The Americans have also fifty lady missionaries in Turkey in Europe and Asia Minor, including Constantinople, Antioch, and Tarsus.

The Presbyterian Church of Scotland has also nearly 200 children in the capital, many of whom are Jewesses. At Broussa Mrs. Bagdasarian, formerly a missionary of the Female Education Society, is conducting an orphanage. While forty-five girls at Oorfa in Mesopotamia, are being taught by a native lady, aided by a grant from the same society.

The name of Mrs. Watson is so well known as associated with the Lebanon, that a passing mention of Shemlan will suffice. In 1856 that lady visited Syria, when her heart was so touched by witnessing the neglected state of the women, that she resolved to remain and open schools for their benefit.

She built a beautiful house, and for a time defrayed the expenses; but the work grew so fast that additional funds and help were needed. Mrs. Watson then applied to the Female Education Society, and Miss Hicks was sent out and joined her twenty-three years ago. Both English and Arabic were taught by herself and Miss Hicks, while a widow lady presided over the domestic affairs. Later on Mrs. Watson made over the whole of the buildings at Shemlan by deed of gift to the society. This school, called by the natives, "The Flower of the Lebanon," has well fulfilled its mission in training and sending forth native school-mistresses. Twenty-eight are now actively engaged in imparting to others the instruction which in many cases has proved able to make them wise unto salvation.

A very satisfactory report tells of nearly fifteen hundred children now (1882), being taught in seventeen schools, dotted over this "goodly mountain."

Mrs. Watson still takes the deepest interest in her Native Training School, but, not content with her work at Shemlan, she opened a girls' school at Sidon. The children come from various parts of the country; from a wild district near Tripoli; from Joon, where Lady Hester Stanhope lived; and from villages in the plain below Mount Hermon. It is a cheering thought that on the very spot where our blessed Lord and Master wrought a miracle of healing on the young daughter of the poor Syro-Phœnician woman, His name is now made known, and His love for woman daily proclaimed.

The work of Miss Walker-Arnott at Jaffa, and her friend Miss Mangan, is one of deep interest, and the medical department has led many to come who had no care for their souls. The report just issued tells of over ten thousand attendances during eight months, the patients coming from no less than eighty different towns and villages in Syria and Palestine.

The excellent schools established by Mrs. Bowen Thompson, and sustained by her sisters, at Beyrout, are widely known. So far back as 1869, three ladies were sent by the Female Education Society to aid in this important work. That society had in 1864 established a school in Nazareth, and afterwards one in Bethlehem, under the superintendence of Miss Jacombs, who had laboured for years at Sidon, and had a good knowledge of Arabic. She was accompanied by Miss Stainton. After a short season of toil in this new sphere, Miss Stainton was called to her heavenly rest in March, 1878. Her last charge to her beloved friend and the native helpers was—

"Love the little children. Teach the little ones of Jesus. Love the poor women of Bethlehem. Love their souls." This earnest worker has been succeeded by Miss Martin. The day school already has between twenty and thirty pupils, and there are six in the boarding school. A native Bible-woman, Leyla, visits from house to house teaching the women.

A late traveller in the East gives a graphic account of a visit paid to this school. The women, in their picturesque dress, seated round their teacher, spelling out of their Arabic Testaments, and listening with profound attention to an address about Jesus.

The following incident is a touching instance of the self-denying results of the reception of the Gospel message:—

In the large Shaftesbury school at Peelton, South Africa, bearing the name of the Earl who so largely aided in its erection, the girls have been taught that "charity seeketh not her own." Miss Sturrock, of the Female Education Society, who, for nineteen years, has there trained hundreds in the way to heaven, told her Caffre and Hottentot girls that an effort was going to be made to lead the girls of Bethlehem to the Saviour, by opening a school. Of their own accord, these children proposed that they should endeavour, by doing needlework and other means, to raise some money to help the girls at Bethlehem. Out of their deep poverty they raised a sum of £3, which they sent with a letter.

As early as 1863, several Christian travellers urged upon the Female Education Society the importance of establishing a girls' school at Nazareth, the Rev. J. Zeller having already one there for boys. As a result, in the course of the next year, a lady was sent out for the purpose.

God has set His seal upon this work, though it has been beset with difficulties. At one time the rains were so long and so heavy that the roads became impassable, and at a season when counsel and direction from home were sorely needed no letters could be sent. The Kishon was so swollen that no messenger could ford it. Then, just as some of the pupils were getting interested in their Scripture lessons, and committing portions to heart, they suddenly disappeared, won over, it was conjectured, by temptations from the neighbouring convent. Still, though sadly grieved, the patient teacher wrote, "I do not quite lose sight of my girls. Penetrating the mysterious lanes of this little city, I find them in their homes, and seek to win back their confidence."

In 1867, Mrs. Zeller, wife of the Church missionary at Nazareth, urged the committee to establish an orphanage there, and it was resolved to respond to the appeal. A murrain at that time amongst the cattle, and scarcity of food, made the poor people willing to give up their children. Soon more children came than could be admitted. One little orphan was brought, with a promise from some relatives, that if admitted her clothes should be provided. This was a step in advance. In 1874, thanks to generous anonymous donations, the last contribution to the building fund was made, and the present handsome stone building was ere long completed.

It is calculated to hold one hundred children, if only funds for their support were forthcoming. At the present time (1882), eight little desolate fatherless ones are seeking admission, while the small sum of £10 a-year will suffice for each.

As the place where the Saviour was brought up, Nazareth must ever possess a deep interest in the mind of the Christian. Its beautiful orphanage, in connection with the Society for Promoting Female Education in the East, built through the liberality of English Christians, is now the most imposing new building in Palestine. It contains sixty girls, and a prosperous day school is carried on. A letter from Miss Dickson, the devoted lady at the head of the establishment, shows that in addition to a sound education, the children are taught to fear God, and honour the Queen.

She says: "You will be remembering my dear children here to-day, I am sure; the one day in the merry month of May to which they look forward with so much delight. Including the men at work in building the wall, the whole number, ninety-eight, are for the first time in the happy attitude of having a little rest from their toil, and a treat in their own simple, rustic manner, in honour of the Queen of England's birthday!

"The flag 'Rob Roy' gave us is waving briskly, as the day is cool, with a nice breeze. I so like the people of this land to be taught, and to remember gratefully from whom and whence they have received their Bibles, their missionaries, their churches, their hospitals, and their schools; the motive that led England to commence and to carry on this; the sacrifice often made for those objects. Hearty, too, are the cheers given for the ladies, and for the Lady H—— de W——, for the gentleman who gave the gates, and for the friends and supporters at large; and as there is so little of change, one hopes that the events of to-day will leave a mark for good to the elders, as well as to the children, of this poor little town of Nazareth!"

Mrs. Mungo Ponton visited the orphanage recently, and has given the following interesting account of what she saw:—"I have been much gratified, after my journeyings in Palestine, to find myself here (Nazareth) for a few weeks, where, among much that is beautiful in nature, in spite of the ban under which this land lies till the veil is removed, I find a moral oasis, surrounded by much that is unproductive, save in evil. Nazareth, that rejected the Saviour, that chased Him from their midst, that would have put an end to His ministry, scarce begun, still suffers in its sons for the sins of the fathers, among whom one finds the hardest types of unbelief and irreligion, so that with the grown-up the task is well-nigh hopeless.

"I find here an excellent institution, commenced some years ago, directed by Miss Dickson, uniting in its object the care and training of orphan girls from the most tender age, principally daughters of Nazareth and the surrounding villages, where they are lovingly brought up by their Christian mother, a lady of wonderful energy and great tact, whose careful management, business qualities, and shrewd and frugal outlay of the means which Christian friends have hitherto placed at her disposal, have been, through God, the instrument of raising up, overlooking the town in which our Redeemer's childhood and youth were spent, a monument to His service, this orphanage worthy in its appearance of its object, and fit to take its place in competition with many in England. 'A Father of the fatherless is God in His holy habitation,' and 'Inasmuch as ye have done it unto one of the least of these, ye have done it unto Me,' are inscribed on its portals. Miss Dickson has, after untold efforts, at last succeeded in accomplishing her desire of making such additions to the orphanage as will admit of her increasing the number of inmates, now sixty-six, to one hundred. Beds, bedding, and even clothing are prepared and ready for this increase, and applicants for admission, some of an urgent character, have to be refused; for, till more funds are forthcoming from the liberality of Christian England, Miss Dickson does not feel herself justified in further involving the institution, as the present number considerably exceeds that for which funds are provided.

"Here it would be well to state that £10 yearly is sufficient for the education, maintenance, and clothing of a girl. Later on, when the ground bought and enclosed for garden produce, and now being prepared for the wants of the house, brings its harvest, a smaller sum may cover the expense; but no one who has not been on the spot can understand well the difficulties to be encountered, happily now nearly at an end, and the opposition to be overcome, before this noble Christian work attained its present proportion. It is worthy of the cause of England, and of the Master. In His name and for His sake let not the petition for help to finish go unheeded."

"This institution may be termed an industrial school, where destitute orphan girls are trained to clean, orderly habits, and in all domestic duties. The Arab mind, through long degradation, is difficult and slow to remember. It is only by 'line upon line, precept upon precept,' that the inheritance of centuries can, as it were, be overcome, which it can never be in their own homes, where lying and deceit, stealing and uncleanness, prevail, and are in general looked upon as virtues. Of course, here the greatest order is inculcated; the children are consequently happy. Each girl has her own number, with which all that belongs to her is marked, clothes, boots, bedding, shelves, Bible, shelf and recess for her playthings and presents, and peg on which to hang at night the clothes worn during the day. They have their white counterpanes for the day, the patchwork ones, made by themselves, for night use. They receive a plain education in their own tongue, Arabic; later on, in English, for which they show considerable aptitude.

"The more clever among the children, who, as monitors, show talent for teaching, are specially trained, so that, with the exception of the four teachers now helping Miss Dickson, she may be said to have always new ones growing up, from whom to recruit her staff or to draft off to other schools, bearing with them the good seed to plant in other nurseries; many of them bear evidence in their lives of love to the Saviour, and all render a loving obedience. There is no servant in the house, as each month a certain number are counted off to perform in rotation the various duties of domestic service, so that by degrees each one gains experience in the various occupations of a well-ordered house, where bed-airing in the sun, baths, baking, washing (consisting of upwards of seven hundred pieces), are done every week. The meals are plentiful, varied, but plain; the children, because of the regularity and of the excellent air on the hills, are in good health. The wheat is ground in their own mill, after being picked and sifted by the girls; then kneaded, is of excellent quality, and when baked into bread most nutritious, not being too white.

"The cutting-out, making, and mending of clothes is also done by the orphans, and some of the elder ones work prettily in their spare evening hours at fancy work. I must not omit to mention that the clergyman's daughter comes to give them a class-singing lesson once a-week, and they sing sweetly a goodly collection of hymns, Arabic and English, so that by the time they have spent a few years in the Home, they are fitted by experience, education, and careful training, to take a much higher and more useful position as teachers, servants, and some getting married, as mothers of families, than ever was possible had they had both parents in their own home. Many a poor and sickly child, brought from sheer want to the Home, and who would have sickened and died in its own, has, by God's blessing on Miss Dickson's careful nursing, become a useful member of society, and an heir of the Kingdom.

"Connected with this work, mention must also be made of the day school, originating in the desire of parents to have their children, not orphans, also instructed, but for which, such is the Arab character, they will not pay. To meet this demand Miss Dickson had two good-sized class-rooms like lodges built, one at each side of the handsome long broad steps leading to the orphanage, which stands half-way up the hill, at the foot of which lies Nazareth spread out basking in the sun. By this arrangement the day-scholars are kept quite away from the house, and communication with the orphans can only be under the eye of the native teacher or governesses during the lesson hours, which close at 4.30 P.M. They have reading, writing, and arithmetic in Arabic, an hour's instruction in English on alternate days, and two hours daily in useful needlework in one of the class-rooms for the very small children; all this brings them in some way under Christian influence, as the classes are opened by prayer and Scripture reading, and closed with a hymn. On the walls are hung choice bright-coloured texts from Scripture in Arabic. The attendance varies from about forty to ninety or more. Marks are given for regularity and punctuality, and the parents seem desirous that their children should benefit, and scarcely any other schools exist in the town or around except the Roman Catholics'.

"The Home is all astir with its little inmates by six A.M.; shortly after, many are in the grounds enjoying themselves, and learning their daily morning text, to be repeated correctly before breakfast; all is fresh and clean, and the long tables spread ready for it. At half-past seven they assemble for prayers in the large upper schoolroom, with its gallery at one end, the morning salutation uttered standing while Miss Dickson enters the room. Far from her first appearance, however, as she has already been here, there, and everywhere, through the dormitories, to see all beds are properly turned down for their two-and-a-half hours' airing, windows open, the dressing-rooms and lavatories left tidy, where are simple wardrobes, in compartments of which, numbered also, are the clean clothes of every girl most tidily arranged. After prayers, which consist of a psalm read simultaneously, a chapter of Scripture read, verse in turn, the Lord's Prayer, and one from Miss Dickson in Arabic, the bell rings again at eight for breakfast; later on, beds are made, then lessons till dinner. After needlework, and from five to near seven, when they have supper, they may amuse themselves. The evening is passed in preparation and work.

"When, through their teachers, I have asked some questions as to what Scriptures have been read, I have been surprised at their knowledge of the Bible, showing that, as far as head knowledge is concerned, they have been carefully taught, and Gospel truths plainly put before them. Of course, much that would present difficulties to an English child, in the similes of the Bible, is, to the native mind, of easy comprehension. We hope, where so much good seed has been sown, that 'the root of the matter' is in some of them. It is pleasant to notice the kindly feeling kept alive by Miss Dickson with the older girls who have left. She seems never, if possible, to lose sight of them; four such were here yesterday from Cana of Galilee. They look on this house as their childhood's home, and like to keep up the connection, coming, after they are married, to see it again, and their kind friend the superintendent.

"The orphans who are in the house, and subscribed for, call their patronesses their 'paying mothers.' Are there any churches, or Sunday schools, classes, or childless parents, who would like to adopt such, or any solitary child who would like to have a little sister? Here God places before you an opportunity for doing a great and lasting good, not only to the body, but also to the soul, of one of His little ones, specially His, the children of Nazareth; and through them, who knows what other blessings may accrue? May He who loved and blessed such bless this notice, and open the lips of His people to pray for a blessing on the work, and also open some hearts to take lovingly to theirs, as He did to His, some of those little ones, is the prayer of one who has visited and witnessed the work."

The tale of Woman's Mission Work would be incomplete without a reference to the Moravians. It is true that their chief spheres of toil have been amongst the squaws of North America, Labrador, and Greenland, or the Hottentots and Caffres of South Africa. But their work did not end there. True to the ancient motto to go to those who most needed them, these devoted women did not shrink from labour among the lofty mountains of Tibet. There, cut off by snow-covered passes from all intercourse with the outer world for six months in each year, these humble soldiers of the Cross have toiled on, and though as yet it is only the day of small things, they have for Christ's sake "laboured, and have had patience, and have not fainted." With the New Testaments in their hands, now through the hard toil of their brethren completed, they have sought to tell their Tibetan sisters of Jesus' love for poor women. The instruction has been accompanied by God's blessing. During the winter schools have been held for the heathen girls, the inducement to attend being that they were taught to knit warm stockings, and paid for their work. Several women have been baptised, and two with their Christian husbands have returned to Ladak, to show in heathen surroundings what a Christian home really is. Easter Day, 1882, their hearts were made glad when a heathen woman at Lahoul, after careful teaching, came publicly forward and confessed Christ by being baptised in His name. "Who hath despised the day of small things?"

CHAPTER XIII.

FEMALE MEDICAL MISSIONS.

HE records even in these early days of the efforts of lady medical missionaries are so many and so wonderful, that the difficulty lies in the selection.

No tale possesses a more thrilling interest than that of the Women's Hospital in Bareilly, in connection with the Methodist Episcopal Church in America, as told by the gifted pen of the Rev. William Arthur.

An orphanage had been established by the wife of a missionary in that city, and when Miss Swain arrived, duly qualified, she began a medical class of sixteen girls. At the end of three years an examining board of three doctors passed thirteen out of these sixteen girls, and certificated them for practice in all ordinary diseases.

"From the beginning, the necessity of a hospital for women had pressed itself upon the attention of Miss Swain. But this was a project demanding heavy outlay. Yet every week brought some fresh token of its necessity. Native gentlemen said that their ladies would not object to go to a hospital superintended by a lady physician. Near to the mission house was a beautiful site for such a hospital, but the ground belonged to a Mohammedan prince, and the price of it seemed to place it beyond all hope. They could only pray, and this the members of the mission had long done. The proprietor was the Nawab of Rampore —a prince who had boasted that the missionaries never could make their way into his city. Yet, as time went on, it became evident that if the hospital, which had many a time been built in the hearts of the ladies of the mission, was ever to be built in brick and mortar, it must be on the ground owned by the avowed enemy of the Gospel.

"At last they were advised by Mr. Drummond, the Commissioner, to apply direct to his Highness for the estate. Probably Mr. Drummond at the same time used some friendly offices, in a quiet way, with persons influential at the Court of Rampore. Instead of their approach to the royal city being made difficult, they found that, through the friendly influence of the Dewan, his Highness had posted horses for them at each of the six stages of the way. Therefore those 'poor beggars,' as Mrs. Thomas calls them, found themselves, somewhat to their own surprise, faring along in a coach and four, with two footmen, an outrider, and regular relays of horses from stage to stage. For the last stage they were joined by an escort of three mounted soldiers. On entering the city gates they were received with low salaams, and the children cried 'Long life and prosperity.' They were driven to a fine house, and magnificently served. At breakfast they counted twenty dishes, and at dinner gave up counting in despair. Two carriages were sent to drive them round the city, and a message came from the Nawab saying that, 'being specially engaged with his prayers, he could not see them that evening.'

"Next morning, after being taken round to several palaces and gardens, they were driven into the gateway of the royal residence. A cannon frowned directly in face of them, and as they passed five royal elephants made their salaams. When they reached the presence-chamber, his Highness rose, smiled, and held out his hand. He seated Mrs. Thomas on his right, next to her the doctor, Miss Swain, and next to her Mrs. Parker, another lady of the mission. After them came the gentlemen, then the friendly Dewan, and the Chief Magistrate. I seem to be writing incredible records of social revolution. That chair in the zenana of a Brahman, on which his wife was told to sit down in his presence, was portentous. And now this giving of honour at a Mohammedan court to the weaker vessel, in preference to the stronger, is no less disturbing to old, established ideas of social order in India. They talked to his Highness of his palaces, gardens, taste, and so forth, while he smoked his hookah, looking increasingly pleased. But there was a great speech weighing on Mr. Thomas's heart, which, his wife archly says, he had been preparing for a week in his best Hindustani, and with his best reasons.

"After a while the Dewan arose and whispered to his royal master. The Nawab nodded assent. The Dewan then gave Mr. Thomas a hint that the moment was come. His wife says that he began 'with as much shyness and blushing as a school-girl.' He said that he desired to procure, on some terms, the estate in Bareilly belonging to his Highness, for the purpose of building upon it a hospital for women. His Highness smiled graciously. 'Take it,' he said, 'take it; I *give* it to you with much pleasure for that purpose."

"Their hearts were all full, their thanks were silently poured out to God. 'We have prayed for it,' says Mrs. Thomas, 'for years; but never absolutely wanted it as a present. And now we have it.' The generous Nawab had their warmest acknowledgments. The gift comprised a garden, with two fine old wells, a great brick house, and forty-two acres of land; worth, in all, three thousand pounds. And all this given when Mr. Thomas had only opened his lips; and now his fine speech 'of no use!' Ah! speeches composed in the heart, with prayers and cares, and hopes and fears, have a strange way sometimes of doing their work without ever being delivered. Such speeches appear now and then to acquire the power of discharging themselves into the breasts of others by subtler channels, without waiting to go by the way of sound.

"Our company of 'beggars' turned their faces again towards Bareilly, crying, 'So we are to have a hospital for women in India!" Was there at that moment in all India another company as rich, as full to overflowing with the enjoyment of the bounties of Providence? Whoever could have read the imagination of the thought of their hearts would have probably seen, alternating with prayers for the bountiful Prince of Rampore, pictures of wan forms regaining the hue of strength, of hopeless sufferers soothed in their anguish, of heathen women hearkening to the never-ending story of redeeming love and "saving health." And they had their hospital. The Woman's Missionary Society of the Methodist Church found them about two thousand pounds. The grounds were laid out, the old house adapted, and new buildings added to the Nawab's bounty. Thus were provided apartments for single missionary ladies, dispensaries, a clinical room, and three separate suits of hospital accommodation, one each for Hindus, Mohammedans, and Christians respectively. One use of the clinical room seems rather uncommon. Native ladies arriving in their doolies, or light palankeens, would be carried right into the room, and, with one curtain drawn aside, would continue lying in the doolie, and there be prescribed for. One young and pretty lady arriving in charge of her husband, it was found that the vehicle could not be got into the room; and there were men about. What was to be done? Miss Swain tried to persuade the poor gentleman that an umbrella would sufficiently protect his wife from unwelcome eyes. But no; he must have two; and so defended she effected the passage.

"After a while the hospital patients numbered fifty,

of whom six were high-caste Hindus. These brought their families with them. One brought three conveyances, with her husband, three children, sister, and no less than twelve servants, besides furniture and provisions. To Miss Swain the husband was not welcome; but the lady said she could not stay without him, 'Their friends would give them a bad name.' One patient said, 'May I not come here every year and stay a while, even if I am not sick? I like to walk out in the garden here; if I walk out at home, my friends and neighbours think I am very bad.'

"After having passed through an arduous season of epidemic, Miss Swain found the fifth year of her service more satisfactory than any previous one. Then her health broke down, and she was forced to retreat to her native air. The convalescence was slow, but after four years of absence she was once more welcomed, very joyfully welcomed, by old friends and new, back to her post again.

"Mrs. Gracey tells us that when the vacancy took place, prayer was made without ceasing by the ladies, that a successor worthy of the work might be raised up. Lucilla H. Green, of New Jersey, had first studied at Pennington Seminary, then taken her degree at the Women's College in Philadelphia, in which city she had further spent several months in the hospital for women and children. Her accomplishments promised a successful career at home. Her spirit hailed the call to a missionary sphere. Like other missionaries, she had learned to sing her way across the sea. With the pine-clad sand-hills of New Jersey fresh in the memory behind her, and the hospital with its dusky occupants rising in the mind's eye before her, she sang—

> "That Holy Helper liveth yet,
>   My Friend and Guide to be;
> The Healer of Gennesaret
>   Shall walk the rounds with me."

"From the spot she gives an account of the two assistants whom she found prepared to her hand, Rebecca Gowan and Bertha Scigler. They had both been brought up in the orphanage. Rebecca spent two years in Dr. Humphrey's medical class. She was now a well-educated, zealous young Christian, losing no opportunity of preaching Christ to the sufferers. She assisted in examining patients and preparing medicines. 'When I am away for a few days,' says Miss Green, 'she fills my place very well.' Bertha had been brought to the orphanage, a waif of six years old, so frightened by ill treatment, that she not only screamed at those who had to deal with her, but bit them. Tamed, trained, converted, she was now a keen, bright student, writing prescriptions so well that Miss Green did not hesitate when absent to leave her register-book in her hand.

"Miss Green gives a full and lively description of her visitors at the dispensary on a single morning. On entering she receives the salutation of the assistants, and of several women seated on the floor. Clean white clothes and bright faces tell her that these are native Christians. Next comes the wife of a rich merchant in costly array, and she retreats to her carriage with great precaution against male eyes. A

Mohammedan woman, with a kindly, trusty face follows. A mother brings two puny children, and holds a branch to prevent Miss Doctor Sahiba from putting any 'evil spirit into them.' The spirit she would like to put in is eggs and milk and meat, but animal food she must not name. Then a low-caste creature wonders if the like of her will be attended to, and goes away happy. Another woman wants to see if the doctor knows anything, and the two have a trial of their wits. One ragged woman, with 'superfluous dirt,' has 'the usual' dozen bracelets on each arm, and five rings in each ear. The clinking of anklets and the rustle of rich dress announce two ladies from a zenana visited every week. A sweet, gentle woman is a native Christian, and 'a jewel indeed.' ('You would feel,' says Miss Green, 'like putting your arms round her and calling her sister.') Some hill women come in blue, tall and handsome. A Mohammedan gentleman brings his wife and children. She will not take a seat while her lord stands, nor will she speak in his presence. When he turns his back she does so, and very winningly.

"Miss Green finds that when asked their age, most of these women say, in a helpless sort of way, 'How should I know?' or 'The news has not yet reached me.' It is said that there are other countries besides India in which news of their correct age has not yet reached the ladies, and in which the longer it is waited for the further does it seem from arriving.

"In Lucknow, where not many years previously all the furies of war had been raging, Miss Monelle found that her character of lady physician opened her way into houses which had never been entered by a Christian. In one touching case she was called to the wife of a Nawab, who for four days had been in critical circumstances, having all the native help available for miles round, but in vain. Accompanied by a lady of the mission and a native female, Miss Monelle hastened over a distance of twenty miles, in part through jungle. At the palace she was led through yards full of elephants and horses, through a court, and finally into the zenana. There she found sixty women, in gorgeous apparel, staring at her from among their trinkets. In the middle of the room, on a low couch, lay the sufferer.

"A messenger from the Nawab commanded that a Christian hand should not touch the Begum till her father had given his consent; and as he was sleeping, they must wait. Waiting in such a crisis, on such a pretext, soon became intolerable. The lady who had come with Miss Monelle, taking with her the native attendant, sallied out of the zenana, and ventured to attack some three-score Mussulman gentlemen sitting in conclave. To her vehement representations they replied that they knew it all, but no one must disturb the Nawab. 'Somebody must do it,' cried the Christian lady, 'the Begum must have relief, or she will die!' After weary pleading, some one did, with trembling, venture to awake the slumbering dignitary. He came forth in rich robes, with gold mitre-cap, and as he advanced the nobles and retainers, parting to let him take the post of honour, salaamed profoundly. But no one dared to speak. They stood 'as dumb as so many oysters.' One can imagine how the blood boiled in the veins of that American woman, to see all this delicacy about forms, and this insensibility to the life-peril of a young wife and possible mother. After a long time they did gently hint that something ought to be done. The great man announced his pleasure that the doctor should report the exact state of his child, and then he could consider the case. The doctor needed not to wait so long. She reported extreme peril. Then came to her the husband in person, to take her professional opinion. Could she relieve the Begum without medicine? She could not promise to do so. 'Will you promise that medicine will positively cure her?' This, again, she could not do. Then fell from the lips of the Nawab a final sentence which was twofold: a sentence for the doctor, of bitterness, for the patient, of death. "To take medicine from a Christian would break caste, and since you will not promise to cure her, she must die." On her way back to Lucknow in the dead of the night, Miss Monelle forgot the wild beasts, forgot the highwaymen, forgot the gloom, forgot all things but God and those hopeless faces which arose before her even in the darkness. She cries out, 'This young and beautiful creature died of caste!'

"Mrs. Parker, the wife of a missionary at Moradabad, had for twenty years prepared in that city the way for a lady physician, by successful practice of her own. She had distributed medicines in the city, in the villages, on the road-sides. She had visited the sick. She had spent days in personally attending those stricken with fever and cholera; herself being several times brought low by disease. 'I have seen the natives,' says Mrs. Gracey, 'prostrate themselves before her,' to procure her help. She had two native medical Bible-women: Shullock, trained in the original class at Nynee Tal, and Jane Plummer, trained in Miss Swain's class at Bareilly. These were willing and capable, and both in the city and villages opened the way into many houses. In one village Shullock had access to every house. When Mrs. Parker visited it during an epidemic, all, both high and low, took medicines. That represents a very great change, and a giving way of one of the outworks of caste.

"But Mrs. Parker longed for a lady physician. At last she was able to welcome Miss Julia Lore, who, after she had taken her degree, had spent a year in the hospitals in Boston. Miss Lore, in addition to house and zenana practice, aimed at a dispensary. She succeeded in obtaining one. Apparently she expected the pretty array of bottles, glasses, books, and so forth to produce an effect. But after spending a morning or two waiting in vain for a patient, she began to reflect that such attractions were not potent with 'the feminine mind of Moradabad.' After a few more mornings spent without a single visitor, she came to feel that, if the establishment was to be called a dispensary, it must be on the principle of taking the will for the deed. Finally, on the seventh day appeared an old nurse with a boy and a girl. Miss Lore records that the first item entered in the prescription-book was Castile soap, which she adds is 'a most excellent remedy for many Indian ills.' From that day a steady increase of applicants converted the dispensary into a reality. The opening up of private houses and zenanas went on at the same time.

"Called suddenly to a woman of sixty, whom she found emaciated and dying with chronic dysentery, Miss Lore had a hope of saving her life, seeing how complete had been the absence of anything like rational treatment. But the old woman would not risk her caste. Not one drop of liquid from impure hands should pass her lips. A single pill she did accept, but never another. Three days after she had been burned on the river's brink, Miss Lore and Mrs. Parker found her three daughters-in-law sitting on the floor, and they did not rise. For this they apologised, saying that custom required them, on the death of the mother of their husbands, to pass six months of mourning, eating only at night, sitting on the floor from daylight to dark and doing nothing. The youngest was a mere girl, with a "wee" baby in her arms. They had all been at the funeral, had bathed in thin dresses, and taken a long walk home, "and made themselves miserable." The eldest, under her breath, confessed that it was a bad custom. In a happier case, though her medicines were at first refused, and her skill obviously distrusted, by the ladies of a really superior family, who could themselves read and did read, Miss Lore succeeded after a while, by doggedly insisting on having her prescriptions followed, and became a great favourite. By helping their bodies a way was opened to their hearts.

"One night at eleven o'clock she was called to a family of the upper classes. Accompanied by her native assistant, Jane, she was led up narrow, winding, steep staircases, through narrow passages, into a low, damp room, dimly lighted and devoid of furniture. On a bedstead about a foot high, with a few rags about her and beneath her, lay a young creature of about seventeen, her life slowly leaving her; no arm to support her, no one to turn to for a word of comfort. Miss Lore made every possible effort to soothe and comfort her. Every time she fainted, the old mother-in-law would hasten off to cry, 'At last she's dead; she's dead!' The physician could hardly get the medicine properly administered. At last the moment came when she had to lay back on the hard little pillow the lifeless head, and at that moment there was not a creature in the room but Jane! Every one of the noisy, helpless, stony-hearted women had run off! Then arose a horrid din; wails and howls, and invocations of Ram, Ram! The white physician and her brown assistant walked away under the stars, reflecting on the want of fellow-feeling they had just witnessed, and on the fact that in a couple of hours the poor young form would be burning by the river-side."

The importance of female medical missions has been lately brought before the public. Many ladies are already engaged in the work, and many more are in course of training. The "Times" introduces the story of the cure of a Hindu princess in these words: "It is one of the merits of missionary societies that they now and then furnish us with interesting information which would not readily reach us through other channels." It then gives an account, the substance of which is as follows:—

The sovereign of a native State in Central India

applied to Miss Beilby for medical attendance for his wife, the Maharani, who had long been suffering from a painful disease. It was impossible for her to see any but a lady doctor. This lady took the journey of fifty-two miles, and remained for many weeks in this heathen court, where there was no other European. By God's blessing on her skill a cure was effected. She was able also to cure many others in the city and hospital. Above all, she was enabled to tell of Jesus and His love to her Highness, who had never before heard His name. When the time came for her to leave, she was desired to go to the palace to say farewell to her royal patient on Wednesday, the 13th of April last. On her arrival, the Maharani dismissed all her ladies and attendants, so that Miss Beilby might be quite alone with her.

She then said she wished Miss Beilby to make her a solemn promise. She was reluctant to do this without knowing what it might involve, when her Highness said: "You are going to England, and I want you to tell our Queen, and the Prince and Princess of Wales, and the men and women in England, what the women in the zenanas of India suffer when they are sick. Will you promise me?"

She explained that it was no social change in their condition she sought, but relief from their cruel sufferings. She charged Miss Beilby *herself* to give this message to the great Queen of England; not to send it through any other channel, or Her Majesty would think less of it.

Miss Beilby then represented the great difficulty

she would have in getting access to the Queen; that with us it is not as in the East that any one can go to the palace and lay a petition before a native sovereign. Besides, she hardly knew what good it would do, as our Queen could not *make* lady doctors, or if made, *order them to go out*.

"But," said the Maharani, "did you not tell me that our Queen was good and gracious; that she never heard of sorrow without sending a message to say how sorry she was, and trying to help? Did you not show me a picture of a train falling into the sea, where a bridge broke, and did you not tell me how grieved our Queen was? Well, it was very sad those people should be killed, but our condition is far worse. If you will tell our Queen what only we Indian women suffer when we are sick, I am sure she will feel for us and help us."

Miss Beilby felt she could no longer refuse to convey the message, if possible. The Maharani next bade her write it down at once, giving her pen, ink, and paper, lest she should forget it, and added: "Write it small, Doctor Miss Sahiba, for I want to put it into a locket, and you are to wear this locket round your neck till you see our great Queen and give it to her yourself. You are not to send it through another." Miss Beilby then said that before she could make so solemn a promise, she must pray to her God to help her to keep it. The Maharani replied, "That that was impossible then, for the carriage was at the door to take her the long journey to the railway station, and she could not go back into her room to pray." Miss Beilby then asked permission to kneel down there and pray. She had often made the same request before, but it had always been refused.

Her Highness had allowed her to read the Bible, and had read it herself, but had never allowed her to pray. This time the request was granted. Miss Beilby then knelt down and asked God that this message should reach Queen Victoria, if it was His will, and that the way might be opened for her to deliver the message, if it would be for His honour and glory, and the good of the poor suffering women of India.

When she rose from her knees, the Maharani said that she had been speaking as if some one else was in the room, but she had not seen her *pray to anything*. She had taken nothing out of her pocket to hold in her hand while praying. " Maharani Sahiba," said Miss Beilby, " when you recovered from your sickness, after your bath, you prayed to the *unknown* God. I have prayed to that God ; only He is my God, *and I know Him.*" It was but a feeble prayer, but God heard and answered ! God disposed the heart of His servant, Queen Victoria, to see her, and listen to her tale of woe.

The Queen having been told by some of the ladies of the court of Miss Beilby's work and message, determined, in spite of difficulties and many engagements, to see her, and hear all for herself, and accordingly sent for her. It was exactly three months after her prayer, to the very day and hour. " Be not faithless, but believing," seemed to sound in Miss Beilby's ears. Her Majesty listened with great interest, asking many questions, and showing the deepest sympathy. Turning to her ladies, she said: "We had no idea it was as bad as this; something must be done for these poor creatures." The locket, with its written message enclosed, was given to the Queen, and Her Majesty entrusted Miss Beilby with a message in reply.

But the Queen also gave her a message which might be given to every one with whom she spoke, on the subject of these poor suffering Indian ladies: "We should wish it generally known that we sympathise with every effort made to relieve the suffering state of the women of India."

In parting with Miss Beilby, before she left India, the Maharani said, in solemn and earnest accents, "If you forget your promise, *your* God will judge you."

Christian sisters, the time is short, "the coming of the Lord draweth nigh." Cannot every one among us, who has tasted that the Lord is gracious, do something more than we are doing for these our suffering and benighted sisters in heathen lands?

The writer's task is done.

Her flowers are gathered, and her nosegay made, and, to use the quaint language of an old writer, little is her own, save the string that ties it.

She has endeavoured conscientiously to exhibit specimens of the labours of women, born in different countries, and called by different names, but all united in the one great object of pointing their heathen sisters to Jesus, the Saviour of sinners. Perhaps the one pre-eminent trait in these workers is their humility. The work is not theirs, but the Lord's. Patient, when no fruit was visible, and humble, when blessed with success, they laboured on. Working in this spirit, and not for the advancement of a party, or individuals, God's blessing is sure to follow. Henceforth let not Ephraim envy Judah, nor Judah vex Ephraim. Let every worker abroad and at home seek to be able honestly to offer up the Apostle's prayer, " Grace be with *all* them that love our Lord Jesus Christ." " Christ is preached, and herein we do rejoice, yea, and will rejoice."

www.ingramcontent.com/pod-product-compliance
Lightning Source LLC
Chambersburg PA
CBHW020925230426
43666CB00008B/1579